BROTHERS

Born to Believe

Published by Full Wits Publishing Inc.,
Suite 250, Unit 14, 4 Westwood Boulevard,
Upper Tantallon, Nova Scotia, Canada B3Z 1H3.
902-857-1900 tel • 902-857-1771 fax

The full line of fine books from Full Wits Publishing Inc. is available at select bookstores and direct from the publisher at www.fullwits.com. For further information, visit our website: **www.fullwits.com**

Canadian Cataloguing in Publication Data

Carter, Butch, 1958-
Born to Believe

Includes 2 separate texts on inverted pages.
Each text has separate cover title reflecting single author.
ISBN 1-894389-05-0

1. Sports — Psychological aspects. 2. Spirituality. 3. Carter, Butch, 1958- 4. Carter, Cris. I. Carter, Cris. II. Martin, Cynthia, 1957-
III. Title.

GV706.55.C37 2000   796'.01   C00-950072-3

Cover photo by: Ron Turenne
Manufactured in Canada by: Print Atlantic
Book layout & design by: Deborah McGowan
First Edition: May 2000

Full Wits Publishing Inc.
www.fullwits.com

BROTHERS
Born to Believe

BY BUTCH CARTER & CRIS CARTER

WITH CYNTHIA MARTIN

personal reflections & inspiration

Full Wits Publishing Inc.
www.fullwits.com

Table of Contents: Cris Carter

To God, my maker and my source.

Preface & Acknowledgements

When my brother Butch first sounded me out about us writing a book on personal reflections and inspiration, my first thought was 'add it to the list.' Both he and I are busy in sports, deeply involved with our families, are active in businesses and in community work. I've long wanted to work on a biography, much like many athletes who constantly get asked how they succeeded. But, I felt this unique concept of combining the thoughts and words of Butch and I into one book, but clearly as individuals, was compelling and just as unusual as our stories. And just as uniquely, we wanted to wait until the book was published before we read each other's work.

   With 25 chapters from each of us on many similar and different topics and issues that affect people of all ages, we felt that instead of reciting off statistics and records, we wanted to focus on giving readers inspiration, mixed with our personal reflections and beliefs.

You'll find many differences between us, but one similarity we share – besides the name Carter and a love of sports – is our unwavering commitment to the service of others.

In giving thanks, I must first thank my source; God. I believe God gives food to every bird, but does not place it in the nest. I believe that everyone is put on this earth to achieve some unique purpose, although many do not know or seek this purpose. I have worked to find my purpose, and I know I was born to believe in myself.

I have also received some other help along the way. To my wife Melanie and my children, I give thanks every day that I get to wake up with you in my life. To my mother, sisters and brothers, thank you for your inspiration and guidance.

*"There are worse crimes than burning books.
One of them is not reading them."*

JOSEPH BRODSKY (NOBEL LAUREATE POET)

Biography Summary

As the second youngest of seven children, Cris Carter was largely raised by his mother and three brothers and sisters, including co-author Butch Carter, in Middletown, Ohio. Cris continues to build on his reputation in the National Football League (NFL) as a star receiver, record holder and award winner. Most recently, he was named the first recipient of the Walter Payton NFL Man of the Year Award for community activities in January 2000, and was the 1999 recipient of the Byron "Whizzer" White Award by the NFL Players Association.

Making seven consecutive trips to the Pro Bowl, Cris ranks fourth in NFL history in career receptions, the second among active players. He ranks second in NFL history in touchdown receptions, 10th in NFL history in total touchdowns and is one of four active players in the all-time top 10. He holds nearly every Viking receiving record, and has broken the 100-yard receiving plateau 35 times in his NFL career, leading the Vikings in receptions for a record eight straight seasons. A dedicated athlete, Cris holds the team record for the most consecutive games started by any wide receiver.

He was claimed off waivers in 1990 from the Philadelphia Eagles, after being selected in the fourth round of the supplemental 1987 draft. Cris earned first-team All-American honors in 1986 and was a two-time Big Ten selection at Ohio State, finishing as the Buckeyes' all-time leader in receptions and touchdown catches. He ranks second in school history and set a Rose Bowl receiving record as a freshman. Cris also scored 1,600 career points in high school basketball before choosing a career in football.

Ordained as a minister off-season in 1996, Cris is active in "Cris' C.A.U.S.E." (Christian Athletes United for Spiritual Empowerment), and the Big Brother-Big Sister program. With college roommate William White and NFL colleague, he established the Carter-White Charitable Foundation and frequently speaks in schools about substance abuse prevention. Cris and his wife Melanie have two children, Duron and Monterae.

Introduction

for Butch & Cris

Before beginning to read this book, try a little exercise. Point to yourself. That's right, put the book down and simply point to yourself. It is unlikely that you pointed your finger at your head. I'd guess that you were pointing straight at your heart. The book that you are about to read was written not from the head, where smooth intellectualizations and clever explanations can be employed. This book, every single page, comes straight from the writer's true self; that which is in their hearts.

It is for this reason that I am proud to introduce you to the Carter brothers' observations on what it takes to reach one's highest level of achievement and personal fulfillment. It is straight from their hearts, aimed directly at yours, where you do all of your living.

Cris, his wife Melanie, my wife Marcelene and I had dinner together a short while back and I listened as Cris detailed his journey from drug and alcohol addiction into the world of spirituality and higher consciousness. I told them about my similar path and how we all seem to go through four archetypes that psychologist Carl Jung described over half a century ago.

As adults, we begin with the archetype of the athlete. Our primary identity is our body, its appearance and performance. We then move to the warrior archetype, when our focus shifts to what we can accomplish and acquire for ourselves. From there we move to the statesman, where there is less emphasis on what we can get and more on what we can contribute. Finally, we reach the archetype of the spirit where we recognize we are not human beings having a spiritual experience, but rather the reverse; we realize we are spiritual beings having a human experience. My personal evolution through these archetypes is apparent in 26 years of publishing 19 books.

During that dinner and in that evening, we enjoyed several hours of stimulating conversation and interaction. As we talked, I felt the most significant accomplishments of Cris' life were not played out on the contrived battlefields of the gridiron, but in his own heart where he faced far more menacing foes and emerged as a spiritual warrior, rather than a mere athlete. I suggested he tell his story around what transpired in his life to bring him through the four archetypal stages.

Sometimes I'm asked what it takes to be a great public speaker and I always explain I believe there are three ingredients that constitute extraordinary accomplishment on stage. I've found that these three elements apply to greatness on any stage, including this new arena for the remarkable Carter brothers.

Be authentic: these two prominent achievers on the athletic stage offer their advice and wisdom to us all. It comes straight from the heart with almost brutal honesty. These two brothers, who came from the most unlikely of settings to emerge at the very pinnacle of their professions, did not land at the top by accident. As an old saying goes, "The elevator to success is out of order. You'll have to take the stairs one step at a time." The Carters tell about each step within these honest observations, but even more important to me, they also tell about their own stumbles and distractions. They are authentic. Their book is a treasure.

Be enthusiastic: the breakdown of the word enthusiasm translates to "God-within." Butch and Cris share in these pages the same contagious enthusiasm they've demonstrated in their chosen athletic arenas. They seem to love competing, winning and emerging on top. This excitement comes through as you read their inspiring personal reflections. This book 'the most important legacy of their enthusiasm' transcends athletic trophies.

Have a burning desire: desire resides in each and every one of us. We all desire to achieve a high level of success. But, a burning desire is unique. It's like having an inner candle flame that never flickers, though the worst may go before you. This is a desire that cannot be squelched or doused. It must be satisfied. These two proud men have demonstrated that rare quality of a burning desire in their chosen athletic pursuits. They have emerged as stellar examples of supreme achievement in both football and basketball. A burning desire cannot be handed from one person to another like a ball. It comes from within and manifests itself, ultimately, as what we often label supreme accomplishment. In the pages of this book, this burning desire comes shining through, fueled by a spiritual awareness of having made conscious contact with God.

Congratulations Cris and Butch! May your words thrill as many souls as have been touched by your athletic experience. As Jesus of Nazareth put it over 2,000 years ago, "Where your treasure is, there will be your heart also." This book is a treasure, because it contains the essence of your greatness. I now know what you meant at dinner that night Cris, when you told me you and your brother were born to believe.

In love and light, Dr. Wayne W. Dyer
Author, including *Wisdom of the Ages, Your Sacred Self*

Addictive Behaviors

Clearly I was an addict. Drugs, alcohol, gambling, sex. There's no denial. What sticks out in my mind is that my descent was a gradual process – not one-time events. It always seemed as if it was just going to end.

The key to breaking addictions is truthfully recognizing the situation you're in and knowing addiction is a very transient and shallow way of hiding your rejection and inadequacies. It depends on the addiction and on the speed you go down. Alcohol was the slowest, marijuana and then hard core drugs.

I always thought that drugs would be part of my life as I was growing up. It was just something people did in my neighborhood. The first time I got hooked was when I got drunk, then I started using marijuana. I did cocaine for the first time at my high school graduation. I thought I was just experimenting and never really thought any of it was wrong. I never even thought about stopping. It wasn't only acceptable, but my friends encouraged it.

Plenty of kids I knew were using drugs at home and if it wasn't marijuana or alcohol, there were prescription drugs. For me, it wasn't so much peer pressure because I'd always been a leader, so I can't use that excuse as to why it all became an addiction. I think I drank because of peer pressure for the first time, but that wasn't why I continued. I thought drugs and alcohol made me feel good and then over a period of time it seemed to shelter me from difficult situations. Later, I understood that I had a lot of pressure during this time from my peers, schoolwork and family that just built up. I did not recognize it all as pressure, so drugs and alcohol seemed to help me before I realized I actually needed them to prop me up and I became addicted. Drugs and alcohol became a big part of my life, and I was using them at least several times a week.

I left high school as the all-time reception and touchdown leader and picked Ohio State as my college. It was pretty much like high school. It was a large school, like a city unto itself and similar to the demographics where I'd lived in Middletown, Ohio. There were some 100 guys on the team, including a couple of buddies from my high school. So, I always found someone who wanted to smoke. I got suspended off the football team at one point, and even that wasn't enough of a wake up call. Having marital problems was what eventually got my attention to make significant changes and get my life back on course.

I met my wife Melanie in the spring of 1987 at college and I was clearly interested in her. I wasn't smoking dope as much because drug testing for the athletes was starting so it restricted my use in season. But, during the season I just switched to alcohol. Besides, when we started to date, Melanie said she wouldn't date me if I smoked. I went through a period of getting around the tests, and all it did was swing me to abuse alcohol. It still didn't click that I had to stop. I'd been doing drugs since I was 15 years old and felt I was able to hide it and manage it.

I was drafted into the NFL in 1987 and managed to hang on

for a few years before hitting a slide. Just before the 90/91 season I was put on waivers and was picked up by the Minnesota Vikings. They saw something in me, but it took me a while to acknowledge what they saw, without the support of drugs.

Drugs do terrible things and affect your performance, your schooling, jobs, relationships and family. My drug use also really disappointed my Mom – she never thought that I would get caught up in it the way I did. And, during this time, I almost lost the most important relationship in my life. My wife had stuck by me and considered my addictions were over. I threw them away and thought I was cured – but I just adopted another addiction; gambling.

Gambling was something I've always enjoyed – just the pure thrill of chance and the feeling it gave me. I was able to pull myself out and able to see the pattern I had been developing. It never got me into trouble and I never bet on football, but I lost a lot of money. But, it was also a social thing. The guys would get together to play and although I was never big on going to places like Las Vegas, I enjoyed playing cards. That was something we grew up with in our family, but Grandma was against it and wouldn't let us play cards in her house. We had to set up in a carport with my aunts and uncles playing with quarters.

As if this all wasn't enough, I think I was still looking for acceptance and validation when I started seeing other women. Sex with women allowed me to escape and it gave me whatever feelings I wanted to have. It was just boredom, lust, fantasy; and so very easy to find. Whatever it was though, it was just sex, the same as if I needed a drug. The women were like drugs; they were not to be seen in public and my behavior was kept hidden. I got a high off of keeping a secret. Of course, Melanie was never to find out, but it all started to unravel. She started discovering more and more and finally, during counselling, I confessed to it all. That's when we separated and we thought it was the end of our relationship. But, we recovered and flourished with a great amount of life-changing faith.

It was in 1993 when I realized there was something major missing from my life. I suffered a crisis of confidence and experienced a long debilitating period I can only describe as feeling intensely broken and fragile. Even though I had fame and fortune, my foundation was missing. I was so broken from a spiritual standpoint, I didn't have trust in people or faith in myself. I had allowed destructive behaviors to be part of my life and both my wife and I were not proud of how we related to each other. Melanie and I started on our journey back to each other on opposite paths. While we each found God at the end of our individual paths, we also found each other again and I overcame my addictions.

However, in understanding I have an addictive personality, I have to recognize when I get caught up in a new activity, to the exclusion of everything else. An addictive personality can be a good thing if it's channeled, as that dedication to football is the same focus I bring to other areas. Whenever I've done something, I've gone after it with all my heart. I like games of chance until I know how to master them, then I get bored with the games. Over the past nine years, I've become caught up with golf and still play occasionally, as it's the most relaxing thing I do.

I actually prefer solitary sports and don't like team sports; an ironic revelation maybe, but when I watch golf or tennis on television, I wish I played those sports professionally. My wife says I can get addicted to a new activity every day. One new activity is fishing and I started that by going one day and then every day for the next four weeks. That's something I enjoyed as a kid that I just drifted away from. It's another one of those solitary pursuits where I don't need people around and one I really enjoy. My son also moves from sport to sport, which I see as gaining competencie.

If a game is on television, I have to watch it but I don't watch it for entertainment or to waste away a few hours. I'm still deconstructing and analyzing plays. That certain high that I used to get from my addictions I don't need as much anymore, it was just who I was at the time. My energy is channeled into other areas now and instead of reaching a high, I want to reach peace. I have a great deal of peace in my family; that is one and the same. But I still need to work on cultivating my relationships as a father and husband. It will always be that way and I accept that as reality. I do this through keeping active, being with our kids and through our faith. I am always in pursuit of ways to exercise my mind and I have a very good imagination.

I think the drug testing in college was a good thing and still is for athletes and others in the working world. With drugs being illegal, I don't see a difference. Drug testing should also be done for people in responsible professions. It's not as if football players are responsible for the safety of people or in charge of people's stock portfolios. But can't say that we want athletes to act like normal citizens, but treat them differently. It's impossible for them to feel the same as others in society when the rules are altered. If a job involves making decisions, especially on behalf of others, drug testing should be done to ensure people are not under a debilitating influence.

If there is one good aspect about using drugs, it's that it makes me who I am now and gives me a reference point when I talk to teenagers. It gives me a tremendous understanding of people and I can reflect on my experiences. I can use it to relate to people and get inside their world. I know how easy it is to get caught up and know how people become addicted. When I look back on it, I used drugs for eight or nine years and lost more than a few of those years. But, I am also not frightened in the dark moments that I will have addictions again. Because of my faith, I can say with confidence God will not fail me. I have confidence in how He permeates my life now.

I still worry about the harm I might have done to my body that I don't know of, and the harm to other people through the influence I had on them at the time, but I am so thankful I came through those addictions with understanding, support and wisdom.

"I thought I could change the world. It took me a hundred years to figure out I can't change the world. I can only change Bessie. And, honey, that ain't easy either."

BESSIE DELANY (DENTIST)

HAVE YOU ABUSED ALCOHOL OR DRUGS OR HAD OTHER DESTRUCTIVE ADDICTIONS?

HOW HAVE YOUR ADDICTIONS HURT OTHERS?

HOW HAVE YOUR ADDICTIONS HURT YOU?

WHAT CAN YOU DO TO GIVE UP YOUR ADDICTIONS?

"Responsibility is the price every man must pay for freedom."

EDITH HAMILTON (AUTHOR)

Authority & Rules

I don't care what you do in life, there are always going to be rules that you don't want to follow. Are some of the rules ancient? Of course. Are the rules overboard? Sometimes. Do they all make sense? No. But, it's important to know that rules are there to help people respect community standards. And community standards are reflected in the governance of the people, the governments we elect and the ideals we respect in each other.

I'm very respectful of authority, the rules we all must play by, and my individual responsibility. Of course people want to express their individualism and often lash out to make a point, but look at life like a game of your favorite sport. If you and the other players did not follow prescribed rules, just how long do you think the game would last?

Football is one of the most highly organized of sports and we have lots of rules. We also have to respect the authority of our coaches and referees. If you deconstruct the game, the players pay attention all the time to other forces so we can best channel our discipline and action. From learning to obey the quarterback and his rhythm, showing up for practice on time and observing off-season training regimens, respect and attention to authority and rules is part of our daily life.

My life is very regimented, based on the authority Coach Dennis Green has over the players and staff. We're going to eat at certain times, lift weights at certain times, meet at certain times and if not, there are penalties if you're late. He lets us know from the very first day that although all of the excuses are probably truthful, none are acceptable. I understand well the ultimate authority over me and the respect that must be given to a coach. Sometimes I might have a different opinion or even different values, but I still recognize that person has authority over me. I never try to defy that authority, as then it becomes difficult to work well within that environment.

I've participated in sports from an early age so I've already had respect for those in authority. It's stayed with me through grade school, high school and college. The better the coaching, the stronger the authority; coaches and teachers are there to help and protect us.

Rules are really norms. The rules are there to help you; rules are not there to hurt or penalize you. This is hard to see when you're young, especially if you haven't been taught respect for yourself or others at an early age. It's tough to see how you fit into the larger picture of a community, with responsibilities within that community. When people are striving so hard to achieve individual greatness or goals, the sense of community and respect for authority or others often gets shoved in the background.

Do we uphold the 'right' to allow a teenager to own a gun because we want to protect the right of that kid, or do we want to promote a safer and healthier sense of community, by saying that using guns to address problems is clearly unacceptable? Although it may be legal to own a gun, authority must be used to protect and personal responsibility must be employed to retain the privilege.

Every civilization needs rules. Rules help a community get along. If you personally have problems with rules, you're not thinking about other people and the effects. For example; imagine you could come to school at noon instead of 9 in the morning, if you didn't have to take a test you didn't want to, or file a report by the deadline. If there were no structure there would be anarchy.

What is true is that the rules actually don't apply to everyone in equal measure. So many people did things and still do things for me because of my name and athletic ability, that it's hard for me to distinguish equality. Something as small as being pulled out of a lineup for a table in a restaurant can really trigger you into believing you're above the norms – even if people change and manipulate things for your benefit, you have to realize that's not the way it's normally done. It's not real life. In the work I do in playing football, it's important to know certain rules apply to me as well as everyone else. But, when an authority figure is able to trust you, there can be more flexibility in the rules. Over the years, I think I've proven myself to be trustworthy, so for example, when I get into the game I may have more flexibility than another receiver.

Similarly, we have high expectations of our children. Many parents serve a disadvantage to their kids in that their expectations seem to be lower and the everyday responsibilities of life are not learned. We see kids with maids and nannies and these kids do not learn to be responsible as part of the family to do such regular chores as vacuum, wash dishes and the other daily responsibilities in life. Those kids, as they grow older, will experience many many daily frustrations as they attempt minimal living skills, not to mention, deal with the larger life issues responsibility brings.

I understand the difference among appreciation, thanks and expectation. When I go to places where people treat me nicely, of course I like that. It's a sign to me of their respect and their appreciation. It's not as if I go to some place and abuse them or their kindness. So many celebrities abuse this kind of acknowledgement and feel they're entitled to special treatment, especially when it's been happening for a long time.

I've always been very opinionated and sometimes that might get in the way of an authority figure, but I understand there are certain time to express yourself and certain times to remain quiet. Respect for rules, authority and people is a two-way street; the more respect you have for people, the more you will gain in return. The more respect people have for you as a person, the more people will respect you as a professional, in the sports world or by being a responsible parent who instills this in a child.

Respect for authority came from my mother instilling in me a respect for my elders; disrespect is something she would never tolerate. It was just natural for me to take that respect I learned at an early age further. Sometimes you will have personality conflicts with people, you'll bump heads with someone who has the same type of personality you have and you might regret your actions. But, as long as you obey laws, act morally, and apply the standards you apply to everyone else equally to you, then you understand rules.

I tell my coaches all the time that I never want them to think they can't tell me something I need to hear, reign me in, or remind me of my place. Going into my 14th year, there's not a lot I don't know. But, I always have to realize that I am part of a team, in football and in the larger 'game' of life.

"I grew up to always respect authority
and respect those in charge"

GRANT HILL (PLAYER, DETROIT PISTONS)

HAVE YOU DISRESPECTED AUTHORITY FIGURES?
HAVE YOU BROKEN ANY OF SOCIETY'S RULES?
IF EVERYONE BROKE SOCIETY'S RULES, HOW
WOULD THIS AFFECT YOUR COMMUNITY?
HOW CAN YOU FURTHER RESPECT OTHERS?

Being Educated

I have to state right up front that I'm a firm believer that a college or university education is not for everyone. There are a number of ways that people can learn, become educated, or master a skill whether it's through a trade school or community college. I'm sure if you go out to dinner at a restaurant, you don't even think about if the chef has an advanced college education, but you assume he or she has received specialized training in food preparation. Similarly you hope your car mechanic really knows what's under the hood and isn't just tooling around.

Life is an ongoing process and the point is that everyone should learn a skill because you have to have some type of occupation to contribute to society. No matter what occupation or profession you choose, you have to continue to grow and appreciate life-long learning. If you went to a doctor who graduated 20 years ago, wouldn't you want him or her to have learned about new techniques and new drugs applicable to your care? Of course you would. In every profession there are always new things to learn.

While a broad education is helpful if you are unsure of a profession, for me going to college was a constant force in my life as my goal was always to become a professional athlete. When I played college football, there was a lot more time spent on football but now the educational system has balanced it out and there's ample opportunity to get a great education. It wasn't until halfway through my senior year that I decided to specifically pursue football, so I had work hard at everything to make the switch and learn the position. College is good for you in that it pushes you to find your way in life. The experience can really put a strain on you to learn, or it can be a holding pattern so you can decide what you want to learn in the future.

Ever since I was a little kid I knew I was going to be a professional athlete. I had a dream since I was seven years old that professional sports would be my occupation. I even remember career days at school where they talked to the kids about what they want to do as a career. I used to tell my teacher that I wanted to be a professional athlete. I had to do whatever it took to get to college to get where I wanted to go, and I needed a sports scholarship.

While the teachers didn't want to dampen my dreams, they did say that I should have something to fall back on. Well, I loved numbers and was very good with math but I was sure I wasn't going to be an accountant. I'm not one to squash someone's hope, but now I tell kids the same thing I was told. I tell kids that if they are going to choose professional sports as a career, choose something as a back up. I still enjoy math and business, it wasn't work to me but I never used it as a bail out.

I obtained scholarships as an amateur athlete when I first got out of high school and didn't look back. The first two years I took classes but didn't like school and thought I was wasting my time. I left college early, after three years, so I could turn professional. School just wasn't that important to me and I could not stay focused on anything other than football. It was hard for me to understand why I needed what they taught me. Now, as an ordained minister, I have taken some theology classes but it wasn't the same as school, as attending the classes was more of a passion for me.

However, I believe there is no excuse for not having a high school diploma. You must have that basic education to allow you to make the best choices for yourself. For children, I think they need special attention and it's essential that early education reinforce the need for continued learning and discovery. And, it's essential to read constantly to children to open up their horizons and create a passion to learn. By having a book or two on the go, you are always expanding your mind, using your imagination to go places and meet interesting characters, and to learn about life.

While I would like my kids to be professionally educated, like most parents, I ultimately want them to be happy and to use their individual gifts to full potential. As long as education is part of their lives and they take advantage of the opportunities it brings, then they will cultivate a desire and respect for life-long learning.

"We must remember that intelligence is not enough. Intelligence plus character – this is the goal of true education."

MARTIN LUTHER KING, JR. (CLERIC, CIVIL RIGHTS LEADER & AUTHOR)

WHAT DO YOU NEED TO LEARN?
WHAT DO YOU WANT TO LEARN?
WHAT EDUCATION DO YOU NEED?
IS THIS A SHORT-TERM OR LONG-TERM GOAL?

"Lord, make me so uncomfortable that I will do the very thing I fear."

RUBY DEE (ACTRESS AND ACTIVIST)

Being Scared

One thing I've learned as I grow older is that everyone is afraid of something or someone. If you let your fears take over, they can take over enough of your life to make you feel that you're the only one who has these fears. You feel what you're going through is faced by you alone. Through the years and through my career, I've realized that everyone is fearful. So no, you are not alone.

What's important is not the part about being fearful, but realizing your own personal fears can be overcome. If you are fearful of the dark – like a lot of kids – the more you become afraid and the more times you're placed in that situation and you're forced to overcome fears, the better you can handle that fear. It becomes part of your make-up and often something that was a fear becomes an asset. You can then use this situation and past experience as motivational tool to overcome other fears.

For example, when I was a kid I was afraid of walking down the street at night. That was through a combination of possibilities; would someone attack me in the rough neighborhood we lived in? Or maybe even worse, was someone afraid that as a young black man I would attack?

I know it's not cool for young teenage boys to say they are afraid – like where a guy thought being home without his parents was going to be a great party time. But, as soon as his friends left, he was afraid. The house made noises or he thought someone was breaking in. We all have certain fears. But as we age, we probably don't have as many as when we were young, as to some extent others had control and comfort over our fears.

Many years later and much more profound for me, I realized I had a huge childhood fear of not living up to the expectations people had of me. The pressure placed on me made me afraid of failure. With my make-up and personality, it didn't seem like pressure at the time. Looking back, it seems I was fearful of not living up to their expectations.

Even now I feel pressure to win the game. I don't want to get any injuries and have my kids watch me fall. But, to be a good receiver, you must overcome the fear of getting hurt. I've seen so many people being hurt and watched the pain it creates in the athlete, but also what it does to the supporting families. So I try to overcome that fear by staying healthy, practicing, and reserving my energy in warm-up. Still, I've been hit hard a number of times and I have been wiped out – you just learn to deal with it as it's part of the job.

For example, receivers don't much like going over the middle to catch a pass, but someone has to do it. The quarterbacks appreciate it because it creates more space if you have someone who can operate over the middle and it's a chain effect so overcoming that fear can turn into a positive. The more first downs you catch, the more opportunities you'll get to catch passes and the more passes you catch, the more touchdowns you score. The more touchdowns you score, the better your team's chance of winning.

My ultimate fear is to become paralyzed – I try not to think about it but it has happened, like in 1978 to Darryl Stingley of the New England Patriots. More recently it's happened and a player has even died. This affected everyone. You try not to think about it but it's real. It's happened and I never want — nor want anyone else — to be in that situation. Football is just a game. For me, because I have stronger faith now, I resist fear with prayer. I do believe God has a plan for me and I'm willing to accept the plan. I would never be able to explain God's reasoning as His ways are higher than ours, and His thoughts are higher than our thoughts.

I've been fortunate in only missing four games in 13 years because of injury, and otherwise I've been able to play through injuries. When my streak of 111 games of catching a pass ended in December 1998, I played with an injured calf, but I didn't catch a pass. For help, I go to the scriptures that pertain to whatever I am going through, for example; scriptures on being timid and on how God did not give me the fear but gave me the power to overcome fear. One of the most common scriptures people find comfort in is Psalm 23, The Lord is my Shepherd, where it says I fear no evil, the rod and staff give me comfort.

I realize what God is trying to say is that people are like sheep. We are blinded as we go through life, so the shepherd is like a staff. Anytime a sheep would feel the shepherd was around they knew He was close. This gives comfort to deal with simple fears like being alone, to know that God will never leave you or forsake you — fears that both young and old go through.

To help my children, I try to explain to them that God is with them and will protect them. They can pray if they get fearful and say the name of Jesus. Non-believers have to find something they can tap into, some spiritual or calming source in which they can take comfort. This might be a certain poem, a paragraph in a book, being in their favorite part of their house or to look at a favorite picture - there are a number of ways someone can gain comfort.

No matter how you deal with being scared — and everyone is

scared at some point – what matters is how you deal with your fears. Try listing what makes you fearful and how you intend to deal with your fears, keeping in mind what you are fearful of today may not be what you are fearful of in the years to come.

"You can't really say enough about Cris Carter. The guy came back after two weeks with a high ankle sprain. Nobody else in the league could do that."

DENNIS GREEN (HEAD COACH, MINNESOTA VIKINGS)

WHAT FEAR DID YOU FACE THAT YOU CONTROLLED OR CONQUERED?
WHAT HELPS TO QUELL A FEAR YOU HAVE?
WHAT ARE YOU NOW FEARFUL OF?
IS THERE A SITUATIONAL FEAR YOU CAN OVERCOME?

Believing in Dreams

I went to a conference and something one of the speakers said struck me as both the saddest and most inspirational words of the weekend. Dr. Myles Munroe, a minister in the Bahamas, was speaking about the unique gifts of individuals. I'm paraphrasing, but he said the richest real estate is not the oil fields of the Middle East or the diamond and gold mines in Africa, it's the land of the local cemeteries, for they hold the unfulfilled dreams and failed hopes of lives once lived.

What that really means is to get out of life all that God gave you the ability to achieve. It means honoring your desires, your unique talents, your ideas and your creativity. We always think our dreams are greater than our abilities. They wouldn't be dreams if we didn't have the ability to fulfill them though. I think when dreams are put into people they are not put into only one person, so it's important to fulfill your dream because someone else might achieve your dream before you do.

I look at it from an athletic standpoint, in that I have trained myself to be the best I can be and I will not settle for anything less than that. There are some other dreams in my life where I haven't put in the same effort in achieving them, but those dreams aren't any harder to fulfill. I just haven't put the energy or focus into those dreams yet, concentrating instead on the one I'm living now. I always thought my career would be great; but that's not ego talking. I always thought I'd be professional athlete and I worked hard and I am experiencing my biggest dream every day.

While I am living a dream now, it's just a path to my real purpose in life. I don't believe God's intent for me was just to be a football player. I could be an owner, a general manager or be a coach. I could also make a contribution in other areas. I always thought I'd be as successful in business as in sports, but I'm just starting into business and finding it's not a natural progression.

Typically, people don't think they can do a number of things well. I don't have the business experience on a daily basis that a person my age would ordinarily have, although I do believe it's never too late to start something new to keep developing yourself. Certain activities are very intriguing to me and certain things are very foreign to me. Even though football is a very visible business, there's a difference between the business of football and playing football, and as I've gotten older I've began to understand more of the business aspects. But, as much as I've been intrigued in business, something else keeps drawing my interest.

Lately I have found I do enjoy providing commentary on television. I have been working at commentating for years and had people tell me I was competent. Maybe they're being nice, but they certainly are supportive. Am I doing it because people think I can do it or doing it because it's a natural progression as an athlete, or something I want to do? Probably yes to all three, but the fact is I have a great time and I'm dreaming now of that role. However, anything that currently affects my workouts and achievement of my dream of going to the Super Bowl is a major distraction.

I've gotten a lot of enjoyment out of broadcasting and it doesn't seem like work. I feel more comfortable now and I don't have any anxiety. I feel as if I'm helping people understand why I love the game. I feel I can tell people what is going on in football and in doing that they'll enjoy the game more.

Someone told me a statistic that I thought could not be true – something like 98 percent of people who watch the games have never seen a game in person. Well, the way a game is seen from the stands is different from the way you see it on television. The game is totally different from where you view it and there are no replays. The game is faster at the stadium, not from the sense of time, but in between you obviously don't get the commentary.

I think the people who know of me and see me on television know I'll bring them information that will help them enjoy the game. I speak in language people understand, in common terms and explanations. I'm not on the level of being so complicated and it's easy for me to translate what is happening. I understand the fans sitting at home who are watching the game.

I also have dreams for my family, my wife and my kids. The day I came home after I first did a commentary, I said to Melanie that I wished she could find something that made her feel that way. I realize it's a strain to be the prime caregiver with the kids and support me. And, given her personality I realize she's not totally fulfilled. My hope is not to try to fix it for her, but I want to help her see her personal dreams fulfilled. If she doesn't, she's not going to be a complete person unless she's able to fulfill the hope and creative ideas which are within her.

I also want to fulfill my dreams for my kids and show them that part of achieving their dreams is fulfilling their potential. I believe if I achieve my dreams I'll be happier and it will help my kids pursue their dreams. If it's my daughter's dream to dance, I want her to have the best dance instructors and go to the best schools for dance. I see many people, who through a lack of fulfillment in their dreams and lives, have seen it affect the raising of their kids; whether it's staying in the welfare cycle, being in a community that is not supportive, or remaining in an abusive marriage. I've also seen many parents, my mother included, who knew there was a better life possible and through the strength they gained from watching their kids grow, knew they had to create a better life where a kid's dream could flourish.

The key is to understand your potential and do something about it, whether it's taking a tiny step or a giant leap toward it. Dreams come true and reaching your dream isn't the end. A person never says 'I've dreamed of this and this is where it stops.' Living my dream of being a professional athlete is not the end of my dreams – it is an avenue to somewhere else. I keep thinking back to those profound words of Dr. Munroe of the failed dreams and just hope that he's not right.

"Can't nothing make your life work if you ain't the architect."

TERRY MCMILLAN (AUTHOR)

WHAT ARE YOUR PERSONAL DREAMS?
WHAT ARE YOUR PROFESSIONAL DREAMS?
IF YOU COULD DO ANYTHING, WHAT WOULD IT BE?
WHAT WILL YOU HAVE TO DO TO LIVE YOUR DREAM?

*"For whatever reason, God has blessed me with the ability,
put me in a position to make these leaps and bounds. I'm
fulfilling my part of the bargain, which is to give back and be
a positive influence on others. That's all you can do; take
what you've been given and spread it around."*

DENZEL WASHINGTON (ACTOR)

Community Service

One of the few things besides football that has fulfilled me is certain aspects of community service. It has largely humbled me in the way football has fulfilled me; mentally and emotionally, in knowing I can share a gift of human connection. In the sports arena I enjoy the hands-on time with the kids and seeing their improvement in athletic ability, but I also get great fulfillment when I visit those who are sick.

The most memorable visit I made was one without any fanfare or any promotion. It stands out in my mind, because it was one child and me. It symbolizes what is right about community service in a very basic human way. Robert Smith, a running back on my team told me about an 17 year old boy in the hospital, who had cancer and was dying. Meeting me was his wish. I went to Columbus, Ohio, to see him and it was truly an unbelievable experience for me. There was no fanfare, no adulation, no clapping – just the disbelieving eyes of a boy who's hero knocked on the door and casually walked in the room.

He really couldn't believe it was me. He hadn't been told I was coming and the look in his eyes was of total shock. He had pictures of me all around his room along with my jersey. I told him whatever he wanted me to do was fine – just talk, sign autographs, take pictures, whatever he wanted to keep him happy and comfortable. He talked about sports and school, and the relationship he had with his church. He talked of the relationships he had with other people. He understood he had only so much time to live and he was excited as the hospital was letting him out so he could go to his graduation. He had such tremendous spirit it made me humble. If I was in his position would I have the same peace? I don't know; there would be a certain amount because of my faith, but I'd probably look back and wish I had done more in my life. So to be 17 years old and realize time was finite is quite different.

He made me understand he was living every day to the fullest. His room overlooked the park and he told me the highlight of his day was watching when the kids would come and play pick-up basketball. His focus had to change from being an active kid who played sports, to the highlight of his day being to watch others. I knew he was going to die, but didn't know he was going to die a week later. His excitement at seeing me, his peace and his humbleness in the face of death will stay with me as a reflection of how one single person can get joy from my ability. And, that's the best of community service.

Since then, most of the visits I do are like these; individual contacts through the Make-A-Wish Foundation or requests from friends. That is truly the ultimate in humility – no matter what I do or accomplish, it's humbling to know that someone is dying and their last wish is to meet me. For the most part, these kids are terminally ill. I've met so many kids and it's hard not to get attached to them.

But far too often, well-meaning people on the fringe usurp our intention to do what is right and what is best for these children. I try to hurry and sign autographs quickly so there is more time for the kids but it frustrates me. I clearly know that nurses, staff and doctors work hard, but if someone was willing to infringe on those few precious moments in that room with that young man, then they are not respectful of the true meaning of community service to others.

So, when I think of this meeting, I am conflicted. Seeing people in a setting, such as a hospital still is a meaningful expression of emotion and hope, but I am torn in that I know hospitals want to obtain some public relations and media benefits out of visits. It helps them showcase their very important work to the public through what the attraction of celebrities can provide, but I feel sad that we need to publicize these children as a way to gain attention. I can't imagine what it would have done to my meeting with that young man if there were television cameras filming us. In the desperate need to fill airtime, compete for ratings or prove our worth, we make a spectacle – and often a mockery – out of the most meaningful of human connections.

I don't want the focus to be on me except for the need my visit illustrates, and that's to show that we are all human at our core. But it's amazing to me that we go into a place for two hours and we may spend only 45 minutes with the people we go to see. A bad part of professional sports is you come off as being a snob if you don't want to sign autographs. But, it has nothing to do with that. I just don't want to sign for adults or someone who might turn around and sell the autograph, when we're there to see the kids. I realize these kids are in a situation we never will understand and I know that's the last time I'm going to see them. I want to make my time count with the ones who will take the most intrinsic pleasure out of our visit.

I don't do events in my hometown because it's my hometown and I like to go somewhere I'm not promoted. Besides, it seems self-serving there.

It is fascinating how people can say negative things about community service, but a lot of times when you try and do something for the community you're not supported. It also takes a lot of work to plan an event and make sure the details are handled. We had a program where each week we invited two kids from inner city schools to attend a game. We were giving four tickets to every game but we had very few respondents. It turns out that the kids in the schools never knew. The principals were responsible for picking two students each, who had achieved certain goals. It was the most unsuccessful thing we've done.

We get asked to take part in so very many events that it is hard to balance and most of the time we have someone from the team scheduling the visits. Once my wife and I thought a scholarship would be a good way of encouraging education and helping kids who were going to college. When I first came up with the idea for the scholarship, all these companies wanted to come on board. I went to meetings but there were stipulations to give matching funds and it occurred to me that they really had no interest in the scholarship. All they cared about was how could they could use my name to their benefit, so instead of matching funds from corporations, we just organized it ourselves.

We sent letters to the athletic directors at each of the high schools in Minnesota. It was amazing to us that the response was so low – maybe we received some 20 essays from high school athletes. Everyone who responded came to a game, met the players, we gave them memorabilia and announced the $5,000 scholarship. We picked one person; a girl from a small town. She was so appreciative and she wrote us a letter after her first year of college that we still cherish.

We try to instill the idea of community service in our son Duron and daughter Monterae. Although they are a bit young to understand the concept of money, we are starting to encourage the value of giving. At Christmas they select two gifts and with the rest of their Christmas money we buy gifts for children who are not as fortunate. They help shop for the gifts and wrap them and we take them to families who need them. Our whole family has learned from that and we have done variations of that gesture since they were small children.

I do think it all goes back to the service you can give to one individual, one family or one community. If you can give money to a local womens' shelter, sponsor a child in a developing country, or be a volunteer at a hospital, it's the caring human contact that counts.

"Service is the rent you pay for being."
MARION WRIGHT EDELMAN (CHILD ADVOCATE)

HOW DO YOU HELP OTHERS?
IN WHAT WAY DO YOU MAKE YOUR CARING COUNT?
WHAT CAN YOU COMMIT TO DO, TO BETTER YOUR COMMUNITY?
IF YOU CAN'T GIVE MONEY, CAN YOU GIVE YOUR TIME
AND EFFORT?

"Self-esteem is something you have to earn! The only way to achieve self-esteem is to work hard. People have an obligation to live up to their potential."

BETTE MIDLER (ENTERTAINER)

The Difference Between Ego & Self-Esteem

I like to think that being comfortable with yourself is something that comes from within by honoring your physical, spiritual, mental, intellectual and emotional selves. Whatever roads you have followed or been pushed along – this is where you are at this minute and you cannot change the past. Given that, how do you feel about who you are and what you've accomplished? It's how you have dealt with your life to this point that I'm talking about. Are you full of hot air and just full of yourself? Or do you feel you have positive self-esteem and are happy to be who you are?

The difference between having an ego and having positive self-esteem is another one of those areas where there is a fine line between the two attributes. I think if you have true confidence in yourself, you have self-esteem. You know your personal power, or as some describe it; a healthy self-image. Everyone has an ego, but, as with anything in excess, too much ego can be damaging. In having an ego or being egocentric, you look upon yourself as the focus of attention and can become self-centered.

Well-accomplished athletes must be selfish and egotistical and it takes a certain make-up to have confidence in personal ability and recognize weaknesses. As a wide receiver in football, a player has to have the confidence that he can out smart or out jump the defensive safety to get the touchdown pass when he's in the end zone. This analogy also applies to a salesperson who's not afraid to do what it takes to get the big contract. But, you have to combine preparation, training, ego, confidence and self-esteem to get positive results. This process starts with honestly evaluating yourself and your shortcomings, faults, failures, and fears. The trick to self-esteem is to marry the characteristics of essentially being a good, content and humble person.

When you're younger you see the ego aspect expressed more. As you grow up, you are trying to define your life and create an identity amid contrasting messages. You're trying to fit in, yet find out who you are becoming and what you think about issues. You have to run with the pack to be accepted, yet be an individual. This is just like being a star receiver on a football team. You have to have ego and self-esteem.

If you start to develop a comfortable sense of who you are when you are younger, and what you believe in, it's easier to deal with threats as you get older. I see this a lot when kids feel they have to drink or smoke or swear to belong to the group. They don't; just some of the vulnerable kids think they have to uphold some tough image. People tend to succumb to peer pressure because of low self-esteem, as the easy thing is to run with the crowd even when you know it's not what you should do. I knew in my heart that getting involved in drugs and alcohol all those years ago was wrong, but I didn't think I had an option then.

I also see it when people make mistakes and don't learn from the experience. For example, if you've been charged with driving under the influence of alcohol, isn't it time you learned something about yourself and to stop with the hot air excuses? True self-esteem here would be to pick yourself up, understand you have a problem and to deal with it, asking for or accepting help when you need it. Ego would be to think you're impervious to causing a bigger problem or to say you just had a hard day.

To some extent, we have all helped athletes create over-inflated egos. People have treated them differently and the athletes think they are special and above being normal. I realize that I'm blessed athletically but I also realize I'm not the best athlete God has created, nor is that important to me to know. I train the same way others train, I just get different results and believe in myself and believe I'm making a contribution to my team. I never thought I had low self-esteem but I realized much of my earlier motivation was to please my family in the normal need to be loved and admired. I think that's to be expected. Since I've gotten my self-esteem at a good moderate level, my ego has gone down and I'm truly happy with what I do in life.

This belief creates the same effect in reverse though. I see this in kids with parents and teachers who tell them negative things. I see the parents who blindly tell their kids they are stupid and up to no good. Then they wonder why their kids grow up with low self-esteem or get into attention-seeking trouble. I think this is a terrible slight on young people as the negative talk eats away gradually at their self-confidence. They then start to practice "self-talk" where they tell themselves they are not good at something and will fail. That's the worst of all – they don't believe in their own power to be positive or contribute to others. I do believe we are all born with some natural self-esteem and belief in our own ability to do things, like when your young daughter turns to you and naturally says, "I can do it myself," when she's trying to tie her shoes. But, much is ingrained from our surroundings, our environment, the actions of other people and even off-hand thoughtless comments.

I think some athletes don't have good self-esteem. That leads back to me always asking what someone's motivation is for doing something. You can't do what we do in professional sports over a long period of time if your only motivation is money. But I see many people whose motivation for money is wrong whether they are in sports, business or in health care. It's amazing how many people I run into who are caught up in the power of money. They trudge away to jobs knowing they hate work and would love to do something else, but feel trapped by an ego need to be the top salesperson, rather than figuring out another way to pay the mortgage. However, our public reward systems are largely based on ego and not whether a person feels good about him or herself. Just because you have a talent it doesn't make you a better person – what you do for a living makes you function in the real world, but just because you're a great lawyer doesn't make you a good person. Just because you're a valedictorian or a television anchor doesn't make you a good person; it means you can perform in a role, but that's not who you are as a person.

You have to believe in yourself and separate what you do from who you are. You know you have positive self-esteem when you can do what you enjoy and not be consumed with the results. Or, when you are more consumed with doing what you want to do, without being worried about the external rewards. You have to believe you have great potential even though you may not be getting the results you want. You have to stay focused on the potential that you want out of your life when situations and opportunities present themselves whether it's luck or your hard work. Many young people have low self-esteem because they don't know what their purpose in life is; they are living day by day and they can't take advantage of life's opportunities.

It must be pointed out to children early in life that everyone has a purpose and they should know early on that no matter how much time it takes, the goal in life is to find their purpose. That's why many people are really unhappy, thinking there is more to life. They have not found their purpose and are questioning their existence. The point is to find what you really believe in your heart of hearts is what you want to do. Many young people know this already, they don't want to be ambitious and may want to play drums instead of going to law school. If that's what someone wants to do I encourage it – but as I said before, be realistic and have a back up plan.

When you read positive affirmations and the encouraging words of people of any age who have faced hardship or blows to their self-image, it helps to see that you are not alone and others have experienced what you have felt. Of course each person is unique and may not feel exactly the same way, but the message to take away is the same; that someone has faced a personal challenge and risen above failure, self-loathing or lack of confidence. At the same time, it is essential to feel sympathy or empathy for others and not have an inflated ego where you think you are superior. Most people are in pain and fragile at various times in their life. It's important to remember to say kind words and remember we are all facing difficult times in finding out who we are in presenting a face to the outside world.

> *"Being powerful is like being a lady.*
> *If you have to tell people you are, you aren't."*

MARGARET THATCHER (FORMER PRIME MINISTER, UNITED KINGDOM)

DO YOU HAVE POSITIVE SELF-ESTEEM AND/OR AN INFLATED EGO?
ARE YOU CONFIDENT AND HAVE SELF-WORTH, OR FEEL YOU'RE BETTER OR MORE DESERVING THAN OTHERS?
ARE YOU COMFORTABLE WITH WHO YOU ARE?
ARE YOU FULL OF "HOT AIR" AND AFRAID OF MAKING CHANGES OR LETTING DOWN YOUR GUARD?

"Never begrudge others for what they have, because you don't know how they got it. Instead, work hard and pray for the things you need and you will be blessed accordingly."

HEATHER EBANKS (RETAIL ENTREPRENEUR)

Doing Homework

People think I just go out and play football. But, they don't see I'm constantly studying and strategizing. I always know what's going on; I know the plays, I watch tapes of my team and the competition. Even when it looks like I'm just sitting and watching television, I'm doing homework. I'm following all the moves and the plays and I predict the action. This focus on the strategy behind the game makes me a better player.

Before a game, I'll go on the Internet and pull up the newspapers from the hometown of the team we're playing. I like to find out the basics of the team; who they are, what makes them special, their philosophy and who's injured. Doing this kind of homework helps me get prepared mentally. It's just the same as if you're walking into school to write an exam or give a presentation at a sales meeting. You have to prepare and learn as much about the situation as you can, because you don't know what information you'll be required to use.

When you get into a situation where someone isn't as regimented, ultimately you force him or her to be undisciplined by applying emotional pressure, and in football, physical pressure. When that occurs in a game, the lack of discipline is going to come out. When I'm studying a defensive back or a safety on film during the week before a game, I recognize that in a crunch time in the fourth quarter, he's going to be even more undisciplined because he's tired. There's one cornerback in particular who is phenomenal and very athletic, but he's not disciplined, so I know he'll have some mental lapses when I play him. While he may not change the course of a game, over the course of a season and throughout his career, I'm able to figure him out. If he was disciplined, he'd be the best cornerback in the NFL.

I've always enjoyed studying – even in junior school I had the discipline. This focus on studying started in high school and grew more intense in college. I had access to weeks and weeks of tapes I could watch to study the plays. I found I enjoyed studying in a way that I saw was of benefit to my life, so the tapes and the studying provided a way for me to learn further skills. You'll focus best on your area of interest anyway, and while some people complain that the scholarship system in college sports focuses on sports instead of pure education, I didn't it see that much.

It's also crucial in other areas I'm involved with now, such as business enterprises. As my character is to be very goal oriented, I use the concept of homework as a way to reach my goal. And, I struggle if I don't always have a goal in mind, which is ironic of course, considering what I do every game is try and reach the goal line.

Every play has a purpose, such as the "Hail Mary" desperation play when it's the last play of the half or the game and you just have a chance to make a long pass. This is a designed play; one guy jumps, one guy waits for the tip forward and one waits for the tip back. I like knowing its strategy and how it fits in with the approach.

I find doing my homework gives me an edge mentally and

physically, which adds up to my competitive edge. If, in my research, I find out a player has had knee surgery a while ago and during the game he gets a cheap shot on me, I'll tell him that if he hits me again I might cut him on his knees during his hit. This kind of knowledge ends up being a psychological advantage also, as talk can affect how we play. It's not all quiet out there.

My wife and I strongly encourage our children to do their homework but the good thing is my wife's standards are so high she even checks the material when I help them! If it's not done properly Melanie will make sure it is done well. Once, when my son had to write a story and use ten new words, I thought what he wrote was fine, but Melanie wanted to encourage him to be a bit more creative and reinforce the distinction between telling a story and just reciting. We tell our children that no one can think for them, so they have to study, because we can't take a test for them.

This reinforces our children's own thinking skills and reinforces the parental role in life. If parents bail out the kids, the kids don't learn. Homework makes up a tremendous part of the learning environment. It's astonishing to us how many parents actually do their children's projects for them, when in the long run, they are not really doing that for the sake of their children's learning, comprehension and ability to think for themselves.

We appreciate a more structured environment for our children at this point and feel we are preparing them for what's to come later in high school and college. By learning to apply life-long thinking skills now, it sharpens their skills for future use. When our children exhibit self-directed learning, we are thrilled.

For example; after one game, my son Duron brought home the game day magazine that had illustrated pictures of all the referee hand signals. I saw it on his desk, turned to that page, for almost a week and I thought nothing of it. Now, ref signals are not something I practice at home. A week later my son came to me, handed me the magazine and asked me to quiz him. He knew all the signals and performed them all, and was just in first grade at school! Seeing that self-interest and study for his own benefit was rewarding to me.

"If everybody in the organization genuinely cares what happens to that organization...it is the most exhilarating, exciting thing you can witness. But, there isn't anything more detrimental to an organization than to have a group of people just putting in time."

LOU HOLTZ (FOOTBALL COACH)

WHAT "HOMEWORK" DO YOU NEED TO DO THAT WILL HELP YOU IN YOUR TASKS?

DO YOUR GOALS AND "HOMEWORK" MATCH?

CAN YOU IMPROVE YOUR DISCIPLINE IN YOUR APPROACH?

HOW CAN YOU HELP OTHERS TO DEVELOP THEMSELVES?

"The tragedy of life is in what dies inside a man while he lives – the death of genuine feeling, the death of inspired response, the death of the awareness that makes it possible to feel the pain or the glory of other men in yourself."

NORMAN COUSINS (PHYSICIAN & AUTHOR)

Expressing Emotion

My biggest display of emotion was not after I scored a great touchdown or missed an important goal. It was at my son's baseball game where I turned into one of "those" parents that can make other parents cringe. I was volunteering as a team coach, and my son came up to bat. I was encouraging him as I would any other child, but then something happened. I saw him as my son and wanted him to do well. It was totally biological. He hit a home run and I was so excited! I didn't know I had it in me but I was jumping and hollering and yelling and waving my arms. Man that felt good! And afterward I was laughing and a bit embarrassed, but that's emotion for you. It sneaks up when you least expect it and you're tagged with that image for years.

Many athletes are quite stoic and blasé as if they expected to score a goal all along. Many, like Barry Sanders of the Detroit Lions, just hand the ball to the referee and with that action you can never go wrong. But I think if you have scored a lot of touchdowns, you have a right to celebrate because you realize just how precious touchdowns are to achieve. But, some do go overboard and it's not right to degrade the team or the opposition. Many athletes in a range of sports are known for a mini-routine when they've achieved a mini-goal, whether it's contrived and part of their act, or random emotion. Chi Chi Rodriguez makes a good putt and he slides his golf club in his belt like a sword, Tiger Williams rode his hockey stick after a goal and soccer player Brandi Chastain whipped off her shirt after a big win. These displays of emotion are largely heartfelt and proud displays of accomplishments, but we've all seen inappropriate displays of emotion with fighting, swearing and just plain tantrums.

Emotional reactions are rarely planned; that's why they are fueled by emotion, so when you look at a winning shot Michael Jordan made in the NBA finals, it's wrong to judge him. I think Tiger Woods is an emotional golfer (besides being an incredible professional), but people unfortunately only like to see his emotion when he's a happy golfer. People expect athletes to be emotional when they want them to be emotional. When he hits a bad shot they don't want to see his emotion, or they comment about it, but all his shots are on public display and we're seeing his personality.

Besides, it's healthy expression and we have to respect it when we see true emotion. We can't ask athletes to show their emotion and then bleed it out of them. We saw this happen in the 98/99 NBA season at a playoff game between the New York Knicks and the Miami Heat. Knicks player, David Wingate, was excited and it was truly great to see. He was on the bench and jumping up to cheer on his team. I'm sure this was his life-long dream and here it was so close. So he was jumping up and cheering like any fan, sharing in his teammates work and encouraging them. He was trying to connect with them as any fan sitting in the last row. I thought that was a beautiful expression of sheer joy.

Then some fan a few rows behind him started yelling at him

to sit down. So he apologized and said he wouldn't stand up, but by the next basket, naturally he was up cheering again. The fan continued to yell at him and watching that made me sad. Here we want to encourage emotion, yet it's always unacceptable to someone.

The players say, "if you haven't played the game you don't understand." What we are saying is that in that particular moment, you have no idea how that other player or I felt; there is no possible way you can understand. You don't understand the parameters of the game unless you've played that particular moment. Even if you think you can understand you are never going to know. I realize emotion, is part of my make-up. I not only play with a lot of emotion I live with a lot of emotion. Anyone can catch passes but very few receivers score a lot of touchdowns and anytime you score seven points it feels good. When I'm getting ready to catch a pass, I'm thinking that whatever I do, I have to catch it. I'm not thinking that if I drop it, I'm going to be booed by the fans. A player has so many things to do in scoring a touchdown. It's not like a home run in baseball where they happen more often and there's nothing an opposing team can do when someone pops it out in the stands.

As I write about in the chapter on *My Relationship with God*, when I score a touchdown, I point to the heavens and pray in the end zone in thanking God for my ability and gift. You may not know what it feels like when you are thrown a touchdown pass with no time left on the clock, but you just know that sets up an emotional response. I like to use the example of Isaac Bruce of the St. Louis Rams who, in the Super Bowl game to end the 99/00 season, caught a 78-yard touchdown pass with less than two minutes to go to win the game. To win the Super Bowl! I thought his response was perfect; he just pointed up into the air.

With my knowledge of broadcast media and general interest in communications, it still is amazing to me how a message can be looked at in a variety of ways; based on the audience, the emotion expressed or not expressed, or even the timing. If we come off the field I might say something, especially if it's been a bad play or if we scored a touchdown. Things have been better over the years in that I increasingly realize that there are certain times to say things. In life you can't just say what you feel all the time and sometimes people can't hear you based on your emotion or their state at the time.

People, opposing players and the media are always watching to see a player's reaction and which emotion they're going to express. By the look on my face, or seeing me yell, people try to interpret if I'm upset, trying to motivate someone, or am supremely happy. I don't think media try to speculate exactly how we feel, but reporters do try to flesh it out and create a story through their interpretation. But when the media print something like that, it's taken as truth, whereas we're often just guessing about the other players. Players are looking for signs of fatigue, fear and dread to gain a competitive edge or advantage. They're watching for signs they can intimidate you and if you show you are in pain, they can use that against you. Therefore, many athletes try to camouflage their emotions. A team can also use this as part of its strategy and planning plays in trying to bluff the other team and players.

Still, with all the preparation that goes into a game, it can come down to an individual matchup – one man on one man. The strategy might be containing yourself or expressing an alternate emotion to throw off the other team. I know different personalities learn in different ways, so I go back and try and understand the individual player and what makes him tick. For example, if screaming is part of your upbringing (and for me it was not so I don't have a great deal of understanding) that may be a way you express emotion – justified or not. But, a lot of that expression of individuality is just being selfish and throwing out any message, rather than expressing your emotion or truly communicating.

I know every player doesn't want to win as much as I want to win and every player doesn't give 110 percent. Like many Vikings, I cried when we lost our opportunity to go to the Super

Bowl because I was shocked we did not advance. At that moment I didn't know if I was ever going to get that opportunity again, but I prayed I would. It doesn't consume me to make it to the Super Bowl, but I would like to say I'd experienced that in my professional career. A very good team is like a family, so emotion and acceptance are all part our profession, and essential components in who we are as individuals, male or female.

Of course, emotion is a crucial part of life with all its richness in living, whether expressing the good or bad, fearful or delight.

"God incarnate is the end of fear; and the heart that realizes that He is in the midst...will be quiet in the middle of alarm."

F. B. Meyer (pastor & author)

How do you express emotion?
Do you hurt people with your emotional displays?
Do you share joy and support people emotionally?
Are you emotionally reserved? Why?

Finding Serenity

The lowest point in my life emotionally was in 1990 when I was put on waivers and essentially sold to the Minnesota Vikings for $100. I was demoralized. I had started to believe what people were saying about me fading and becoming washed up so young. I was fumbling my way through a life filled with pain, expectations and temptation. I had lost sight of myself and what made me happy, and was far from being content.

I realized I had some deficiencies as far as my character. I know many young people have the same struggle and believe I was no different from anyone else, albeit my struggle was public. I could understand why people killed themselves and the despair they are driven to feel. It was as if I was on an elevator going to hit bottom any second. I kept wondering how far the elevator was going to drop before I punched the emergency stop button. My elevator was fairly high, in other words, due to my professional success, I had a long way to drop and it would be a very public fall. Hitting bottom for me was almost losing my family – that's when I started to lose my identity.

I know there are people who lay down and sleep through the night, content with themselves and their entire life. I don't know how they do it. There are people who are naturally serene and I wanted to find that serenity that had eluded me. When I finally started to use my professional skills to help myself, I began to change. What muddies the waters even more, is that my wife was going down her own path, as I write about in *Intimacy*. When I hit bottom, I looked in the mirror and saw my father. I realized I was heading down his path of not taking responsibility for decisions. One of the things I learned was that I had to start with pleasing my family to find true serenity. I feel grateful every day that I was given a new start and the Vikings believed there was something left in me, when I didn't believe it myself.

Sometimes, when faced with the hard decisions, you try to tell yourself you're not who you are; that you are that way because of other influences. Maybe you had a difficult childhood, not perfect parents, or were disadvantaged. So, that's life. You have to understand you are responsible for yourself. You cannot change anything in the past that's happened to you – but you can control the future. I decided that I could control me. I could not control being put out on waivers and being sold for $100 but, I could decide to change what was expected of me.

Without the serenity God allows me or the contentment from my good family life, I would not exist. It's like walking down the road holding someone's hand and they step into a pothole. Do you let go of their hand or wait until they step up and rejoin you? I can regain my step just by knowing God is my source and by looking at my wife. And that serenity is with me daily, whether we win a game or if I pray when we don't win a game. That serenity is with me when I pray through the bad times, which allow me to experience the good times more fully.

To have serenity, you must be thankful every day for the joys you do have and for the gifts of the world – however insignificant these seem. Instead of trying to cut someone off with your car, let that driver into traffic. Open a door for someone or really watch the sun go down and experience the glory of the world. You must encourage serenity in others, practice kindness and caring and be thankful for the simple daily joys in living. First, though, you must be good to yourself and those closest to you.

"Always demanding the best of oneself, living with honor, devoting one's talents and gifts to the benefits of others - these are the measures of success that endure when material things have passed away."

GERALD R. FORD (FORMER PRESIDENT, UNITED STATES)

WHAT GIVES YOU SERENITY OR TRUE CALMNESS?
HOW DO YOU IMPART THIS TO OTHERS?
HOW DO YOU AVOID GETTING CAUGHT UP IN THE
DESTRUCTIVE ASPECTS OF LIFE?
HOW DO YOU ENCOURAGE THIS CALM IN OTHERS?

"If I don't have friends, then I ain't got nothing."

BILLIE HOLIDAY (SINGER)

Friends

True friends are those who suffer all your partially expressed thoughts and who still understand you, those who know the difference between your complaining and your real pain and those who, with an easy smile, quick remark, or patience, have the ability to lift you out of your low spirits. Like most people, I have a lot of different levels of friendship.

I'm not the kind of friend who's going to call all the time or talk on the phone every day. I just don't, whereas my wife and other people I know think nothing of picking up the phone for a good long chat – even if they're going to be seeing that person a few hours later! The people who I am friends with, I'm very good friends. I'd say about half of the people I like spending my time with are in athletics in some way. That's similar with many other situations; the people who are in your profession, business or school program tend to better understand the peculiarities, complexities and strains. That gives some immediate common grounding.

My friend and trainer, Ron DeAngelo, says I have a wall around me much like everyone does, but my wall is a little higher than most. He says I can read a person inside and out and I think he's right on. I feel I've made enough mistakes that I can tell who is genuine and who is not. As pro athletes, we have people pulling at us for all sorts of reasons so it's hard to develop true friendships. And certainly if you're into drugs or alcohol, that's worse, especially if you have notoriety, wealth or influence as people are drawn to you because of those attributes. Substances coat your emotions and your perceptions and you can put layers and layers on top of the act of who you really are as a person and a friend.

When you're growing up, it's easier to develop friendships because you are really trying friends on like clothes. As you age and move through different periods, you see if people fit your style. You are really lucky if you can carry certain friends with you over the course of your life. I think girls make friends easier than boys because they talk more and make deeper connections. Boys seem to settle for less in friendships compared to girls, maybe making more random connections through shared experiences such as sports. I had a lot of friends growing up, friends who were very athletic who I spent a lot of time with and several friends who didn't participate in sports. As far as ethnic background, I had an equal number of friends who were black and white. Racial lines or ethnicity was never an issue.

I noticed a change in my friendships in high school and I wasn't very selective. I didn't understand until much later that certain people only wanted to hang around me or to be seen with me because I showed ability and was successful in sports. I realized that I made a few mistakes in not understanding the nature of those friendships; that some can be one-sided or disingenuous. I also realized that my true friends were not those who encouraged my use of alcohol or drugs. Some people are very vulnerable and it's easy to fall into the path of someone who doesn't have your best interests at heart. I know first hand that there is always much pressure to fit in, but true friends would have tried to help stop my slide. For some kids, these false friendships are destructive and can lead to terrible behavior, such as crime. I have no friendships with people I knew in high school now, largely because of the distance and that our interests have changed.

As you grow older, what you expect from friends changes. In college I surrounded myself with "yes" men. I think that I subconsciously selected friends and acquaintances who matched my personality in trying to reaffirm my low self-esteem. I tended to select people who made me feel better, who'd say things that I wanted, stroke my ego or sometimes blatantly lie. Well, it carried me for awhile, but I got a lesson in who my true friends were. When I went to college, most of my friends were football players and given it was a large university, a couple of buddies who went to my high school were also there. That initially made it easier.

As I went into professional football, sheer distance weeded out the friends. The first four years I was in the pros, old acquaintances still acted as if I was their best buddy from college. One man I met who I played against was William White. William was in the NFL at the time, and soon became my closest friend. Our friendship has endured many tests. He's still in the NFL so it's different from other friendships, as we understand the distinct pressures on each of us, so that's one way of making a deeper connection.

I can say that currently, this is the only time in my career that I've considered the coach to be my friend. Dennis Green has been head coach of the Vikings for eight years and I'm mature enough to handle a friendship with someone who is in his position of authority over me. I respect him and the job he has to do, and like most friendships, it was a gradual development over the years. He's always respected me. In football, with trades and new people each year, building strong friendships is often difficult. To me, he's always a coach, but sometimes he's like a father. Since my father was not around much when I was a kid and my brother Butch became my confidante, it's maybe a natural continuance with the guidance Dennis gives me. I know I can call him and talk to him about anything.

Maintaining friendships is also difficult when your life changes in other areas, such as if you get married or your economic situation changes. It causes a tremendous amount of strain to continue relationships when a friend's economic situation changes for the better, as I found in the sudden expectation that I would pay every time a group of us went out on the town. I can afford to pay, but after a while, a person can't help but feel taken advantage of if they are always covering.

Now I find it's tough to be friends with many single people, as I tend to have more in common with those who have children. There is something about the perspective of having children (and of not being able to stay awake all night anymore!) that changes a person's outlook and focus. It's tough to have children and cultivate friendships with people who just want to hang out. Plus, other parents grasp the shift in your priorities and actually take pleasure in hearing about your child's little achievements.

The friends I tend to cultivate are people with good morals who are family oriented, from any background. My friends now are very established in their businesses and their lives and I would consider them to be everyday people. My friends are successful in what they do. That doesn't mean they are necessarily wealthy, but they are successful. My friends push me, keep me settled and there is a healthy amount of mutual respect among us.

I only have a couple of friends who are really involved in football. Those who are my friends accept my personality and go with the flow. They understand how I think and accept me the way I am. For many friends, even if I haven't seen them in a while, I can pick up the phone and we pick up right where we left off. But, just as anyone, some may think they are my friends who may not be and be someone I consider an associate or acquaintance.

My wife is my best friend. Melanie really helps me more than anyone else. I feel as if I can tell her anything. We were fortunate when we were going through a rough period in our marriage that we had good friends who supported us and gave us the perspective to stay together. And, we have always had Christian friends before we became Christians ourselves, as we admired what they stood for and felt they had good morals.

"At the end of your life, you will never regret not having passed one more test, not winning one more verdict, or not closing one more deal. You will regret time not spent with a husband, a friend, a child or a parent."

BARBARA BUSH (FORMER FIRST LADY, UNITED STATES)

WHO ARE YOUR TRUE FRIENDS?
WHAT DO YOU DO TO MAINTAIN THE FRIENDSHIPS?
DO YOU HAVE FRIENDS OF DIVERSE BACKGROUNDS?
HOW HAVE YOU HELPED A FRIEND RECENTLY?
DO YOU SEEK OUT NEW FRIENDS?

"Give your brain as much attention as your hair and you'll be a thousand times better."

MALCOLM X (ACTIVIST & LEADER)

How Society Judges You By Your Clothes

I don't dress to impress anyone but myself, but in saying that, I also respect the situation and dress for the occasion. I have a few reasons for deciding how I dress and why looking good has become important to me. I'm also not obsessive; I don't spend an hour in front of the mirror primping. I dress according to how I feel. I pick and choose what I want to put on.

I feel just as comfortable in a suit and tie as I do in a pair of shorts and t-shirt. Wearing a suit is not work for me, especially as I feel it's a sign of respect and a good impression to fans. In a post-game interview, I realize that a certain amount is coming across to people through my appearance. I feel like I'm going to a job interview and it shows my respect for the general public and when they see me, I want to look nice. It shows, I also have respect for myself.

It's also a reason why I never give interviews in the locker room. I never do an interview half-naked, with the eye black on or my hair not brushed. I learned that from Michael Jordan. Because of the potential interview and because in effect I'm going to work and then leaving "the office," wearing nice clothing is a transition from my home life to work.

I wear a suit to the game and even if we lose, dressing up makes me feel good. It feels good to me and it lifts my spirits but it's not a new thing since I've been playing professional football. I've always dressed as well as I was able to afford since my college days. I was aware of quality in clothes and felt it was a sign of respect to invest in myself this way. People might think it's because I have the money to spend, but that's just me and my teammates know it's me. I am very conservative and because I also work in the business world on various projects and enterprises, I realize there is often an unspoken code of dress and it's important to me to meet on business terms.

I realize how clothes do define people because on the teams I've played on, the white players wear jeans and t-shirts and they don't have to think so much that someone will judge them. But for me, and for most blacks, it's a sad reality that some in society do judge people by their clothes and image.

It goes back to me feeling like football is my profession. It's important to know when to be casual and when to dress appropriately. If you go for a sales job interview and you wear a baseball cap, ratty t-shirt and jeans, don't be surprised if the person doing the hiring doesn't take you seriously. Even though you are trying to express your individualism, there are times you must learn when to turn it on and off.

As an athlete, dressing nice also breaks any perception of the "dumb jock." It helps stops people from thinking we are just uneducated jocks. People often say to us after the game that we look nice and to me that is not a compliment. It's as if they expect nothing else of us. It's true with any profession – it's just that other professions may not have as great a public exposure. The tendency now that I'm older is to dress more casually. I have a great acceptance of myself and for the most part I'm not meeting someone new to me that I feel I need to impress.

I also talked with my wife early on about not wearing jeans to a game, as unfortunately people begin to form impressions about others also through their partners. My children are even catching on as to the appropriateness of dressing nicely. My wife and I go out on a date once a week. She was shopping with my daughter who was five years old at the time. Monterae saw some fancy strapped sandals and looked over at Melanie with one of those knowing looks and said, "Now these would be great Friday night date shoes!"

"I base my fashion taste on what doesn't itch."

GILDA RADNER (COMEDIAN)

DOES THE WAY YOU DRESS CONVEY A MESSAGE?
ARE YOU DRESSING FOR OTHERS OR YOURSELF?
ARE YOU PROJECTING THE IMAGE THAT YOU WISH?
ARE YOU DRESSED FOR SUCCESS?

"Many times you are a role model for people you don't even know — live your life accordingly."

BRENDA J. LUDERBACK (SENIOR EXECUTIVE)

The Inspiration of Role Models

Throughout my early life, my role model was my older brother Butch. Besides being my father figure personally, he was such a great athlete. As I have gotten older and come into my own, there's not a lot of people I would say are role models for me now. What I do is take parts of individuals — male and female — and blend them together to get what I need for inspiration.

I have not met too many people who, from top to bottom, I thought could be perfect role models for me. I've seen tremendous qualities in people and try to replicate the good aspects, but I realize people are human, with fears and frailties. This is comforting to me, as if someone looks to me as being a role model, they need to know I am just one man. I spend a lot of time in prayer with other professional athletes trying to understand God's words and every day I pray to make a positive impact on someone's life, asking God to not let me get in the way.

People need to understand the difference among exhibiting behaviors worthy of being a role model, being a hero and in having a specific talent that is admirable. I think parents, media, peers or other influences don't stress the differences enough. Just because we see people on television, it doesn't mean we know that person as a friend. Just because a famous actress appears in a movie and then is seen in a store, it doesn't mean the role and the person are connected. While we might admire an actress for her talent, we really don't know the woman she is, whether her role is that of an evil person or the heroine. A particular role she has played may come to mind, rather than understanding her as a real person who just wants to buy a pair of shoes without being hounded.

As a society, we like identification. We like to classify, to put labels and names on people. Even in our own minds we like to put a certain description on things or people. We think it helps to understand them. But it does not; it simply objectifies people and lessens our understanding of him or her as a whole person. Just because you are this month's hero you are not a role model. They are two different entities. I think for the most part people use the term "role model" as a buzzword.

A role model is someone you'd like to model your life after, someone with character such as Nelson Mandela. His whole outlook on life and his ability to keep a positive attitude during all those years of imprisonment in South Africa is a great example. He projects dignity and integrity and gentleness. He shows internal attributes that are significant and worthwhile; that you can grab hold of and say you'd like to model yourself on – not just fleeting external attributes. There is also much debate in sports circles about whether athletes are or should be role models, as many don't want the pressure and inherent responsibilities. It's hard to always be watched in public for one slip up or transgression.

The characteristics that impress me most are common role model attributes: honesty, the ethics of their business interests, how they respect the gift of their life, their expression of this gift in their career, the way they relate to their spouses and their general outlook on life. I also look at what people do for enjoyment, if they are groomed, how they carry themselves in public or how they act under pressure.

I don't think it's a healthy thing to have a real person as an obsession. I've had sports role models and the people I enjoyed watching most were those who made their effort and talents appear graceful and were so competent that sports looked easy for them. But, I don't think I revered them as icons. Even in my house now, besides in my office and a small exercise room, a visitor would never get a sense that I play football. I don't have stuff displayed everywhere in the house. I know who I am and what I do.

As public figures, often in the limelight, sports figures tend to think what we do is who we are, but for me, football is just my job. I play football but that's not just who I am.

People also need to realize there are different role models for different people. Outrageous or scandalous characters may not be role models I would choose for my children, but I do recognize they are role models for others. When basketball star Charles Barkley said he was not a role model, he was absolutely correct and he should not have been faulted. He is not a role model for my little boy growing up. As a parent, I point out people who can be role models, but all of that is trivial if I am not a good role model to my own son. As far as the pressure of me being a role model to others, it is hard as it's really a full-time job – you don't always know who's watching or the effect. While it's hypocritical to be a good person in public and not in private, there are higher expectations on public figures. I want to be a good role model for the way I live and who I am, not because I play football. I want to lead a normal life sometimes. And yes, that includes taking out the garbage at home.

I want to go places with my kids and not have attention directed at me because of the job I do. For example; I will not sign autographs in front of my kids, as I want them to see me as their father. I want them to feel like children and I don't want them to feel any less of a person because all the focus is on me. I'm going to be with those kids for the rest of my life, so I am not a star, I am their father.

I want to blend in and do my own thing – which might be nothing or be very active – but I like to have my choice. In certain instances, I've lost the ability of being an unrecognizable face. I understand that, but I have never gotten used to the attention. If I'm seen as a positive role model, that's one good thing, but if people judge everything I do, that makes me nervous. When I won the Walter Payton NFL Man of the Year Award in January 2000 for my community work, I felt very honored to be considered a role model among my peers. To be given an award that was named after such a tremendous man as running back Walter Payton, especially as the first recipient, was a humbling experience for me. Walter led his life even for people he didn't realize were looking to him as a role model. I think young people are looking for role models and we can make an impact and a difference in people's lives. Rather than an endless loop of a fight of the week replayed on television, it's refreshing to see good life choices are recognized.

Melanie and I were talking about role models as I was writing this and she said her goal is for us to be good role models to our children. Later I asked my son who his hero was and he said, "You're my hero, Daddy," which of course just melted my heart. I then asked him who were his favorite sports stars and admit I was thrilled to hear him say I was his favorite football player. To me, that's the best thing about being a role model – the opportunity to be the consummate role model in my child's life.

"If I'm more of an influence to your son as a rapper than you are as a father you got to look at yourself as a parent."

ICE CUBE (RAP SINGER)

HOW DO YOUR ROLE MODELS DIFFER FROM ANY HEROS?
DO YOU ADMIRE SPECIFIC TALENTS OR ADMIRE THE
WHOLE PERSON?
DO YOU PERSONALLY WANT ADULATION OR TO BE RESPECTED?
HOW CAN YOU ENSURE YOU ARE A GOOD ROLE MODEL
TO OTHERS?

"Love is best felt when one's eyes are closed. But, love is best given when one's eyes are wide open."

AFRICAN PROVERB

Intimacy

When you're a football player or sports star, you don't get asked a lot about intimacy, nor is it something you just randomly talk about. It's sort of like getting asked how I balance my career and my family life; people don't. Women get asked how they balance life all the time, but people just assume men have it covered. For intimacy, if you're like most men, you'd rather pound your thumb with a hammer than talk about it. Half the men have no idea what it is, a few do, and the rest are probably scared to talk about it. They think intimacy is confessing to their buddies that they like an unpopular team.

I'm still learning about the difference between intimacy and sex, and learning as I age. While major life events – and we've had our share – strengthen the intimate bond between my wife and I, I think small things that we each do builds intimacy between us all the time. Intimacy is like many experiences or skills – if you don't use it you lose it – so you also need to nurture it and do simple things like holding hands, kissing goodbye, and saying 'I love you.' People need to focus on the little things that give each other happiness and make them feel secure within the relationship.

Another way to encourage intimacy is through conversation and really talking to one another about how you feel. Talking with each other in real life is rarely like romantic movies. It really is hard sometimes when you're close or in love, to have a conversation that is testy or difficult. It's important to talk through it, and to state what you want and need in your relationship, and even to discuss the tremendous differences in what you think is intimacy. One guy may think it's romantic and builds intimacy to take his wife to sporting event and for the wife it's to go to ballet.

I started college in September 1984 and met Melanie in the spring of 1987. I used to see her around at college and I sensed there was something different about her. She was knockdown gorgeous and I couldn't resist. I was 21 and she was 20 years old. She was a commuter student who came in every day, but her friends lived in the dorm next to mine, so she used to visit and spend time hanging out between classes. Between the dorms, there was a loading dock where the football players used to hang out and we used to see her coming by and would talk to her and her friends.

Initially, she thought all the athletes were jerks, but then one day she came over by herself and I started a conversation with her. That was the first time she got a sense of what I was about; I had been trying to get her attention and I didn't know how to approach her otherwise. The more I got to know her, the more I got to believe she was the only women I had met who could handle me and my personality. She simply had the qualities I wanted. Mel always had a great sense of where she was going and I knew after a very short time that she was the woman for me.

For Mel, the first time she saw me on the loading dock alone when we talked, was the first time she saw me without the protective group of friends. She saw potential in me and realized that underneath all that junk ego there was a nice person with a big heart. She had a rule that she didn't date athletes, but she thought I was a nice person after that first private talk. I used to try to tie into her schedule to get to where she was. I asked her to lunch and she wouldn't go. After a few weeks of begging though, thankfully she finally succumbed to her hunger pangs.

We were both seeing other people and Mel had just come off of a long-term relationship with someone. When we started seeing each other exclusively we were at lunch and someone came up and asked me for my autograph. So I signed the autograph and when I looked at her, she looked shocked and asked me who I was. I made a humble comment of 'you don't know who I am' and she said that obviously she didn't. At the time she knew I played football, but didn't know to what magnitude, she just knew I was on the team. She did not know the trouble I'd been in before; she didn't know anything about me except what she saw in those few weeks.

We had an on and off relationship for two years. I wasn't settled enough, as after we met, I went into pro football three months later so it was a young relationship between two young people and a lot of distance.

In June of 1989, Mel was graduating and interviewing for a job during on-campus recruiting. She was planning on taking a job in Philadelphia. I was in shock and didn't want her to go, so I went to her graduation the next week. I knew I was going to lose her and had to make a decision. I asked her to marry me and we got married in February 1990. Mel got cold feet before she walked down the aisle, getting so tense that her Dad stopped her and told her she didn't have to get married. That's when she started to cry. I saw her crying, so I started crying. She forgot about her tears and started wondering what was wrong with me, as people didn't really know that emotional side of me.

I didn't know if it was the right decision then and we were able to overcome our problems, but the first five years of our marriage was hard. We had to learn marriage was not about being selfish, it's about sacrificing for the other partner and so then we started to focus on that aspect. It wasn't so much our young age that made marriage hard in the early years, it was also my addictions. My life was turbulent and if I had any uneasy feelings, I suppressed them with alcohol and drug abuse.

Like any couple, we have faced hard times and down times, happy times and endearing times. The overriding thought is that each time we faced some issue or shared something, we become more intimate and more committed. I believe these events reinforced our life choices and our decision to stay united as a couple. We held the pressures of the world at bay, with a banded effort that had less to do with the rings on our fingers than the attachment in our spirits.

If we were all honest with ourselves, we would look at our spouses and say we don't know them perfectly. I still struggle to know my wife even though we've been together for 13 years! We're still learning about how to be open with our feelings. I'm still learning that when she tells me something, I have to understand she's not trying to tell me if I'm right or wrong, she's telling me how she feels.

Now, we focus on God first, our marriage second and we learned to develop our relationship outside of kids. This is very important. A couple needs to plan special times such as a regular date night, which does not have to be costly at all – but just getting out for a walk so you can talk about other issues than how the kids are doing. When you have children, it is important for the kids to see you have an intimate relationship that does not include them. My wife and I are proud to show we love each other in front of our children. We tell each other we love each other all the time and we kiss and hug a lot and our kids laugh and act grossed out.

We are thankful that our kids are older and they see our relationship now and not how it was a few years ago when they were young. Profound events change lives and what happened to us was intense but it also strengthened our bond of intimacy.

After a long struggle as individuals and as a couple, we opened our hearts and our lives to God – each on our own path, but in consideration of each other and our children.

As I wrote in *Addictive Behaviors*, I had a difficult time in the late 1980s and early 1990s. This time also tested our intimacy. As many know personally, it's not just the addict who suffers. it's also the spouse and the family. During this time, Mel went for counseling on her own to find herself again – not to reconnect with me. I had already moved out of the house and part of the reason I left was that when she came out of therapy, I realized that she really didn't need me. Our counselor, Betty Triliegi, tried her best. She was an angel in disguise who tried to make Mel understand just whom she had married. Alcoholics rarely marry another alcoholic because they need someone else to be in control to make things better. Mel understood that whatever I had been dealing with was not over, that further tests would just come in stages. Mel viewed this time as being my problem to work out, not hers. In her mind she could not understand why I didn't just stop the behavior.

We had always gone to church; we went every Sunday and when I went to church I felt we were living our life the way we were supposed to. But, we were just going for show, out of duty and responsibility. Monterae was not even a year old and Duron was two years old. Mel had accepted Christ into her life when she had found out what was going on with me. She was pretty broken up and her girlfriend, Daphne, called saying, "you have tried your way and not done any better, now will you accept God?" Mel was so broken and resigned, she agreed.

So, Mel went into a center for a week of therapy where they relied on a 12-step program that stressed your higher power. By accepting God into her life, Mel learned she could depend on Him. When she came out she told me our marriage was not working and she did not want to pursue it. Staying in the same home wasn't productive and we did not want to argue in front of the kids, so I moved out.

When I came to visit, it was hard on all of us. Our daughter would dart over to me as if she hadn't seen me in a year and I'd take our son everywhere I went. I think I was always a great father and Mel agrees, but just being a father wasn't enough and just being a mother wasn't enough for Mel. We needed to be a family again. That's when we realized we needed help together and needed to do the best we could for our children.

I knew I needed a relationship with God and potentially losing my family is what woke me up. During this time, Keith Johnson, who is the Vikings team chaplain, preached a message to the team and at the end of the session, I found I couldn't leave the room. I was crying. He didn't know me well and I didn't know him – but I began to explain to him what I was going through. I had so much pain and hurt within me. I explained to him I wanted to be happy – that was my sole pursuit. I had to get that peace to allow me to be the father and the husband I dearly wanted to be. I knew what the right way was, I just could not yield to it.

A few days after this breakdown, I gave my life to Christ and went to the same center Mel had been at, so I could participate in therapy. It was during that week that I started realizing how much I had been acting like my father. I looked in the mirror and I saw my father's face and what he represented with his lack of responsibility to his family. He had not been a good influence and I was convinced I wanted to be better than him, so that thought gave me the incentive to come back home.

I called home and told Mel I had one of those life-changing experiences, which she knew was actually initiated before I had left. I told her I was going to come home. She was concerned about me leaving the structured program early, worrying if I had really worked things out, rightly saying the solutions weren't all that easy. But, she sensed something had changed and I needed to be home, so I left. I came right back home and we decided it was going to be a slow process. I had only been gone a couple of weeks and because I'd been traveling so much and with our schedules, it really didn't seem as if I had been gone long.

If you have different relationships, jump from person to person or are always searching for Mr. or Ms Perfect, you're never going to be happy or experience the joy and the feeling of being at home in your soul, that being intimate allows. It's impossible to be intimate in a true way otherwise. My wife and I discovered that being in love is not enough to remain intimate with each other and with God's love, we will continue to safeguard this irreplaceable feeling.

"A life without love, no matter how many other things we have, is an empty, meaningless one."

LEO BUSCAGLIA (EDUCATOR & AUTHOR)

WHAT IS YOUR DEFINITION OF INTIMACY?
HOW HAVE YOU CREATED INTIMACY WITH ANOTHER PERSON?
HOW DO YOU STRENGTHEN THAT INTIMACY?

"I always joked that it was time to stop playing when I had to be helped off the field. I'll always miss football, but I'm not going to let it dominate my life."

CHRIS SPIELMAN (SPORTS COMMENTATOR & FORMER LINEBACKER, CLEVELAND BROWNS)

Making Decisions

I have always been a leader and always been one to decide what we're going to do, whether it's making a split-second decision as part of a game, or making a decision at home with my family. Whether you are making decisions for a team, a business, just yourself, or your family, you have a lot of day-to-day responsibilities to juggle. The crucial thing to remember is you are moving forward. As a society, we have to realize that just because a person may have great athletic ability, it doesn't mean he or she has a great ability to make decisions. Because a man can do a 360 degree windmill dunk, doesn't mean he understands that the last drink is one too many. Because a man can run a 40-yard dash in 4.2 seconds doesn't mean he knows how to make appropriate decisions once he gets home.

When you look at some of the football players choosing to get into trouble, what's most distressing is that you look at people who have a tremendous opportunity with their standing or image to make a difference in peoples' lives and they blow it. We're not talking about 17 or 18 year olds making bad decisions. We're talking about men who should know better. We're talking about college-educated players who, for the most part, who have been in the pros at least two or three years. They are making childish decisions despite all the support programs, training and educational resources available to us in the NFL. At the annual three-day seminars for rookies preparing them for a career in the NFL, situations and decisions are discussed. In admitting my problems years ago, I'm happy to lead some of the discussions. The NFL also has a type of "refresher course" for veterans and constantly reassesses these programs. That was the sad thing when I started making bad decisions; there was all this help available around me and I wouldn't admit to needing help until I decided to accept it.

Although I know consensus management has been in vogue in recent years in business, for the life of me, I don't know how companies can operate when you have 20 people sitting around a table in some committee meeting trying to make a decision. It seems ludicrous and a big time-waster. Many meetings are productive, but when decision-making is done by consensus, making an actual decision can drag on and people just plan another meeting. I think that process to include everyone just frustrates those who move the company along; those who make decisions and stand by them. I'd rather see someone stick out their neck and state just what he or she think will resolve a problem and why. When the offensive coordinator, line coach, quarterback coach, and the receivers' coach meet to plot a game plan, they each have a specific task for particular games, and don't have the luxury of time.

It goes back to authority. As a receiver, the decision is not in my power, it's the quarterbacks, but I have a certain amount of influence over the game during the course of a week. When they put in a game plan you can't pull it apart. But, there are certain times when you can offer an opinion on the plans being made –

maybe we can do this play a little different to make it successful or do a play in a different formation. Simply, the best decisions I can make are to ensure I'm healthy and practicing hard.

In the context of football on the field, the players respect decision-making even if they believe that a player can't do something or just can't describe a move in the way they may see it. People do trust me and have a great deal of faith in my decisions so I don't have too many people second-guessing me. A receiver's decision-making is limited compared to the quarterback who makes the decisions on the field.

I used to have a difficult time making decisions. A lot of times I was willing to compromise to make peace, but now I feel that as long as I do the morally right thing and be fair, I'm doing well. People have to realize that whatever decision they make, they are going to live with the good and the bad, so maybe that's why people tend to be frightened of deciding, or pass on decisions because then they're just passing off the repercussions. I do take the time with homework and my studying of the plays and the games in preparation, so I'm satisfied to live with the consequences. But, you have to prepare yourself for hearing the inevitable "I told you so" that you'll hear from anyone who cares to comment, whether they've been in your shoes or not.

Now if you ask my wife's opinion, she'll tell you I'm decisive on social occasions, which occasionally can be a bad thing. I can be indecisive on a lot of things, but when it comes to doing what I want to do, such as the restaurant to go to for dinner, I'm very decisive. If there's a group of us going out and I want to go to some place in particular, I usually don't consult anyone; I just make a decision. My friends know this and now don't even question it – they just accept me, but they do tend to kid me about it.

As far as my family life, as the man of the house I have to make some decisions and my wife may not agree with me. Admittedly, these tend to be simple decisions. But, we always make joint decisions on the large decisions in life and I can't imagine not consulting my family. I'm lucky to be a long-term player on the Vikings, but when you are traded around a lot, it's hard on the family. Although families have no say in a trade, moving should be a family decision. When NBA player Antonio Davis was considering offers to play in Milwaukee or Toronto in 1999, he asked his children. His children thought it would be cool for him to play in Toronto; the team with the raptor on the logo. If that makes his kids happier and feel they are part of the decision, great. It makes them feel consulted, and shows their father appreciated the input.

When you make the decision to leave sports, you have a bunch of memories, but you'd better have money saved. The people who graduated with me 14 years ago are into their careers and climbing while mine will change. I have to choose a second career and if I'm not careful, everything I've learned in my first career will not help me in my next career.

The one thing I realize is, in all the decisions I make, I have to do right by people. I can't make a decision that's going to just be for the benefit of me and to the detriment of other people; whether that's as a family member, as a father or an athlete. Although I can certainly be a procrastinator, you won't find me waffling over what play to make or what movie to see.

"Nothing is more difficult, and therefore more precious, than to be able to decide."

NAPOLEON (RULER)

CAN YOU MAKE INFORMED DECISIONS?
DO YOU HAVE THE CONFIDENCE, EDUCATION AND
KNOWLEDGE TO MAKE DECISIONS?
HOW CAN YOU IMPROVE YOUR DECISION-MAKING,
YET CONSIDER THE CONCERNS OF OTHERS?
HOW DO YOU ENCOURAGE OTHERS TO MAKE GOOD DECISIONS?

Manners

I find that good manners and common courtesies are something that people tend to learn early in life or not at all. A lot of what is learned comes from training my brothers and sisters and I received at home. I was lucky to have a firm footing as I did get this training early and throughout my childhood. My mother would ensure we were courteous and practiced proper manners.

Butch was very polite growing up and became a great example to me, not only as to what my mother taught us, but how my mother and her family instilled those values inside of us. The three main concerns my family instilled in me were the basics: having respect for other people; regard for other people's property; and a heightened respect for our elders.

I don't believe youth today are getting a significant amount of that type of training and I can't say I'm overly surprised by the way some kids behave. I see adults who are rude and the kids see that behavior, so it's hard to teach them. It seems as if we've lost that basic understanding of the courteous role manners play in social relationships. Since many adults don't have proper manners, it's not surprising the kids don't practice good manners. I mean even small courtesies such as opening a car door for someone, letting people out the elevator before you, or standing up when someone gets up from a restaurant table.

I'm really thankful when people go out of their way for me. I still address people as 'Sir' and 'Ma'am' as I think that's a basic sign of respect. And that's what manners are also – basic politeness as to how you wish you were treated. You can't underestimate the value of a thank-you note; my wife is always writing those and of course, our kids write notes to thank people for gifts. These are just common courtesies and manners of which everyone should be conscious. Manners and courtesies are a way of positively communicating your respect of others and setting expectations of how you wish to be treated. Being polite never goes out of style.

It's appalling to me to see kids disrespecting their own parents, because you just know they're not going to have respect for others or their peers. It has nothing to do with who they are or self-expression, they are just badly behaved. Many parents instill this in their children by promoting they have to win at any cost and that they should stand up for themselves at all times. There's a big difference in instilling confidence so a child feels they can do well and encouraging him to butt into a lineup to get an autograph. One of the best compliments I get is from people commenting on how well behaved and respectful my son and daughter are. They can still express themselves individually, but in manners there is no negotiation.

I find it offensive for a child to call me by first name. This comes from my early-engrained manners to address an adult by "Mr." or "Mrs." or "Sir" or "Ma'am." I ensure my kids address their friends' parents like that as well – they even call their babysitter, "Miss." Although they see football players routinely, they are even to address them as "Mr." Long-time friends of ours such as Jake Reed, who's another wide receiver, they call

Uncle Jake!

Although my children are young, good manners are now something that's instilled in them. All we have to do is little checks, such as reminding them to not say, "what?" when I call them. The best example of their training is when they are going to a friend's house and my wife starts to say, "Mind…" and they chime in "your manners!" We do notice differences in our children. Duron is aggressive when he's playing sports but in life he's passive. He would let anybody get in front of him. Monterae would be first to tell us she's next in line. Still, you can't set children on a path and not keep on the path.

Jim, a neighbor of ours, admires that quality in us as he says we've really helped him reinforce the importance of good manners with his son. Kids do watch other kids and pick up a lot of actions through others. We hear about the bad behavior that is replicated, but this is one example where good behavior is also picked up from peers. Jim told us he appreciates Duron's politeness. Before Jim didn't notice it in his own son and it never bothered him before. Now he can see a big difference in the small actions and courtesies emerging. It's in this way – person to person and child to child – that the value of having good manners is reinforced.

"If a friend is in trouble, don't annoy him
by asking if there is anything you can do.
Think up something appropriate and do it."

EDGAR WATSON HOWE (JOURNALIST & AUTHOR)

DO YOU PRACTICE GOOD MANNERS?
HOW DO YOU TEACH OTHERS ABOUT THE
IMPORTANCE OF MANNERS?
HOW CAN YOU IMPROVE?

"What the mass media offers is not popular art, but entertainment which is intended to be consumed like food, forgotten and replaced by a new dish."

W.H. AUDEN (AUTHOR)

Media Relations

I believe athletes have a responsibility to talk to the media, as the newspapers, magazines, radio and television all translate sports to the fans. It's important to work with the media to ensure what is portrayed is accurate and fair. But there is a downside. Because I'm beamed into peoples' living rooms and am the flavor-of-the-month, it doesn't make me approachable in a bathroom at my kid's ball game.

It's not a legal requirement, but practicing media relations is your connection to the fans. While athletes have to control their image to the media, they also realize there's an unspoken partnership and essentially the athlete's job is to help the media do their job. From the standpoint of the team's desire for good public relations, you also want to do your part.

There's a myth out there that all media is bad and out to get you. The reporters may not be your friends and you may not want to develop close relationships, but there are some very nice people in the media. As I have gotten to know reporters, for the most part their writing style is based on their personality – if they have a confrontational style then their writing will reflect that. The media is very good when they don't already have a story in mind, another agenda or a predetermined angle.

In sports, we're generally blessed in that there are beat reporters; specific reporters who cover individual sports such as football and build up an expertise. The reporters have unique personalities and a newspaper may have two or three reporters on the same sports beat. This helps the reporter, the media outlet, the fans and the team as the reporter develops a knowledge base and there's continuity with ongoing stories. A coach or a player doesn't have to go into explanations on basic rules, for example; the reporter already has a good understanding.

If a reporter is a genuinely balanced and curious person, their commentary reflects that balance. I'm human, and as with associates and acquaintances, there are certain people in the media who are closer to me and with whom I prefer speaking. But, sometimes you are better off if you don't talk to the media, such as when the story will be just based on the reporter's opinion or they ask you to speculate on what could have happened.

I try to manage my relationships with the media. I only do a certain amount of questions after the game, maybe 15 to 20 minutes and then I'm gone. You just start repeating yourself or just spout off clichés that aren't interesting. I don't do individual interviews that often during the week. It's too taxing and with my schedule and priority to be with my family, it's just hard to fit in. Plus, the interviewer is often asking just the same questions over again from game day.

I tend not to get misquoted and misinterpreted. There have been occasions where media take things out of context so you have to always clearly state what you are doing and always stay on the record. I never go "off the record," telling media something I really shouldn't divulge.

If they want tape record what I say, that's fine with me as it's easier to prove any discrepancies. I know people who are interviewed are often advised to tape their own interviews with media so they have a ready copy. But, if someone makes me out to look bad on purpose, then that will limit his or her access to me in future.

I think that some people are too accessible, both in sports and just in the general issues of the day. A team might have a great player who's soft-spoken and relatively quiet, yet a guy who's a loudmouth is being interviewed. If media try to talk to a player every time there's an opportunity and a player is just running off at the mouth, the older players know media are just trying to use the younger player as a quote machine. That player eventually gets repetitive and people get tired of only hearing their perspective. Maybe it has got to do with the attitude that you have to jump on every opportunity to talk about yourself, but I think it's overkill and boring. I don't think my kids need to see me every time they turn on the television.

Sometimes media want information or they'll ask me questions about someone else. I try to avoid those comments as you can't win. If you try to speak for others, you'll get grief. If the quarterback has had a lousy game, I just can't go to the media and say he played badly. I've learned as a player that I'm not the team spokesperson. That's the head coach's job. I have to be tactful and maybe can allude to that, but there's a difference between the facts and the truth. The truth is I have to help keep this team together because we're on a journey and me stating destructive comments is not going to help the team. That's also a sign of respect for my teammates as individuals and as members of my team.

It's a thin line as there are certain things I can't or won't say. I'm normally very frank and candid of how I played as I can control that, but we're just not in a position to say what we want to say all the time and have to be tactful. We have to respect each other as teammates and publicly support each other, just as in a family where you shouldn't air out your problems to strangers.

We have team public relations people to help, but to learn how to speak with the media, you just have to get out there and make some mistakes. With media exposure comes public exposure, which leads to interference during private times. All athletes and public figures struggle with the public's accessibility and a person's right to privately enjoy a dinner out or walk with their friends. We know the fans are appreciative and support us, but sometimes it is overwhelming.

However, media and public exposure has now made me a totally different person than I really am. Being a public figure unfortunately makes me withdraw from everyone. I have a tendency to walk with my head down and try and be inconspicuous. It's hard to judge when an athlete is approachable, especially when we seem so accessible and the media take us into homes. But now, if one of our children has to go to bathroom when we're in a public place, my wife will take them because people have routinely even approached me in there. There are not many things worse than being surrounded when you're in a bathroom.

I realize people recognize me and know that people think they can say anything to public figures. Some people are fairly nervous, they want to identify with me, or they may say something pointless. I understand a lot of it is nervous energy and they just want to be able to say that they talked to me. But it accomplishes nothing really. It seems the greater accolades in your public life, the more people think they can infringe on your private life. It's a role I have to play, but I don't want to accept it because it's not normal. I accept it's going to happen, but I don't have to carry on a 30-minute conversation with a guy in the next urinal. It has nothing to do with fame or recognition, it's common courtesy to be respectful.

I used to have a lot of time for people and I try to acknowledge people, but lately I've started being short because I just want to be able to do the things a normal person does when I'm out. It's so much more difficult when I'm with my children

"Cris Carter is one of the most quotable and accessible of NFL stars, and consistently grants time to print and television reporters, both locally and on a national level. While Carter does not suffer transparent or silly questions well, his responses are almost always honest, revealing and thought–provoking. His experience and role as elder statesman within the team affords him the platform and the vantage point to make insightful observations on a wide variety of topics."

DON BANKS,
CNN/SPORTS
ILLUSTRATED

and they don't understand why fans pound on the car or scream. I see the terror in the eyes of my kids as I try to explain and they try to comprehend that people are not trying to hurt us.

The teams all have media relations staff who work constantly to assist in whatever the reporters need and I try to be available when I can. Generally, I can say that my beliefs about good media relations are based on nothing more than good communications; be timely, fair, honest, and accurate. Besides basic considerations and respect, there are a few other things I've found helpful. I try to break out what I want to say in short sentences, have three or four main points and give credit to others.

One thing I learned early is not to fill in pauses in the conversation, as you may say something you regret. If you are in a position where you deal with media, just follow a few basic guidelines from my experiences. Nothing is off the record, don't talk for others, don't speculate on "what if" questions, keep your answers short and above all, have something to say! And always, save a copy of the article for your family.

"Many people feel compelled to watch the local news every night, when it is often just a listing of crime and catastrophe. If you aren't a criminologist or a fireman, this is probably superfluous information."

RICHARD SAUL WURMAN (AUTHOR)

DO YOU THINK WHAT YOU SEE OR READ IN THE MEDIA IS ACCURATE?
HOW DO YOU DISTINGUISH BETWEEN REAL PEOPLE AND MEDIA CREATIONS?
DO YOU EVER GET THE FEELING YOU KNOW TOO MUCH ABOUT TOO MANY ISSUES COVERED IN THE MEDIA?
DO YOU NEED TO KNOW HOW TO HANDLE YOURSELF WITH MEDIA?

"I've learned from personal experience that what Jesus taught me was true: the greatest sense of fulfillment we can find here on earth comes not from fame or fortune but from serving and doing things for other people."

DELORIS JORDAN (MOTHER & PRESIDENT OF THE
MICHAEL JORDAN FOUNDATION)

Mentoring – Being a Mentor

When you become a mentor, it's not as if you sign a consent form agreeing to help someone. It's often more of a moral duty to help others. You realize that when people are placed in your life and you must help them for a reason, because you've been helped in your past.

And, it can be tough. You may doubt yourself, wondering what you've got to give or you may be self-deprecating, but the important thing to remember is that someone can learn from your experiences, just as you have and can still learn from others. Being a mentor is a full-time commitment. You have to be able to say things that might upset the person, you have to push the person and you have to answer your phone in the middle of the night.

It was a bit different for me because I was strongly mentored when I was a young kid, but the ones I mentor are now grown men. They're not malleable or impressionable. They've been having success the way they've been doing things and they don't necessarily want to accept someone being close to them. They already have habits that have been established for a long time and sometimes it's difficult to take guidance. The longer someone has been doing something on his or her own, the more difficult it is to get around that and offer valuable guidance. But, that's often when they need the most help. Given that I live in two states and travel frequently, I'm not part of a formal mentoring arrangement, and with a young son and daughter, I now want to spend more time with them.

After I changed my life in 1993, I had something to give other people. In some respects you become more guarded as everyone wants a piece out of you and the commitment is sometimes difficult because there's so much going on in your life. My life is an open book to whomever I'm involved with and they need to see me in all aspects of my life for me to be of help to them.

Mentoring for me wasn't part of any structured program, it just evolved. I've had periods when I have been asked to help someone and it's not been a long-term relationship. I'm in a profession where people come in and out of your life quite often, so sometimes you might only mentor someone for a year or two. So, you really have to try to do what you can in a short period of time, as you often don't know how long they're going to be with you.

Over the years I've been helping out wide receiver, Randy Moss. He was a perfect person to be matched up with because we play the same position and the first year it was helping to get him settled. There would be so many things he was going to need me for and we just had to spend a lot of time together anyway. We are together eight to ten hours a day. Football can be a very emotional business and when you go through different mood swings together you can get to know someone quite fast. I also was so comfortable with my life and career that I didn't mind spending a lot of time with him. We each had experienced many of the same pressures with substance abuse, so I could impart some wisdom.

Randy is such a good listener and one thing I realized with this was that my approach was 'this is who I am, I'm not your father, I'm not your brother, but I'm your friend.' I never decided to mentor him until we decided how the friendship was going. I really didn't think I could be a mentor and not be friends.

I never thought of the effect that his ability would have as any detriment to me playing football. I thought the role I could play in his life was much bigger than me just playing football – I honestly did. I have never compromised information based upon the thinking that it might make him a better player than me. I can relate to him because of situations that he's been involved with, in that he comes from a very small community, because he's a tremendous athlete and we have enormous mutual respect.

"He plays the biggest role of anyone," when asked what Carter means to him. "(Other players) are important, but I play off this man right here. Cris is the main guy."

RANDY MOSS, WIDE RECEIVER, MINNESOTA VIKINGS (SPORTS ILLUSTRATED, JANUARY 18, 1999)

The relationship is very good and very open and I give him a lot of space. He is still trying to find himself and still very much a friend, but we are from two different eras as far as what we do socially. He's single, I'm married so I spend a lot more time in family pursuits.

Another mentoring relationship that rapidly evolved into a strong friendship is Jake Reed, who was traded from the Vikings after the 99/00 season. We've been playing together for nine years and if Jake and I were discussing something, Jake could also help Randy. It's a great relationship all around as sometimes the stresses of life in professional football can be overbearing. We ate with each other, traveled with each other and talked with each other. Jake is very quiet and very different from who I am and it is a nice mixture.

Mentoring helps people translate the larger world into their world. It extends the idea of community and offers support to someone as they make their way in a larger community, no matter if it is sports, school or the business world.

"In every man there is something wherein I may learn of him, and in that I am his pupil."

RALPH WALDO EMERSON (AUTHOR)

IS THERE SOMEONE WHO COULD BENEFIT FROM A MENTORING RELATIONSHIP WITH YOU?
LIST WHAT YOU HAVE TO OFFER.
HOW CAN YOUR TALENTS AND SKILLS BENEFIT SOMEONE ELSE?
DO YOU HAVE THE COMMITMENT?

Mentoring – Having a Mentor

I've had many people who have helped me over the years, but I think a true mentoring relationship is someone who instills certain values and a confidence level in you; someone in whom you have a strong level of belief as to the positive effect on your life. Being a mentor is not telling people what they want to hear; it's guiding them through what they need to hear.

The thing I now recognize is the timing that my mentors had in my life. I believe they were all in my life for a purpose at the time. Sometimes you don't think a mentor is good for you. You may think they are just plain crazy. But the fact is, at certain points in my life my mentors did things and with certain styles that helped me.

When I was in grade 5, my brother Butch was the most popular athlete in the State of Ohio and reached the All-American basketball team. He was in the midst of making a decision on where to go to college. He was my early mentor in life, including in athletics.

My homeroom teacher was Mac Knepshield and he was the one who pointed out my strength in math and made it interesting for me. He made it fun for me but also gave me difficult work to do to challenge me academically. He was also funny and seemed to have so much confidence in himself, which was inspiring to us because as students we had little confidence in ourselves.

Mr. Knepshield was one of the first teachers to encourage a balance. He wanted to encourage me athletically and academically. He instilled in me of a sense of my own identity and didn't want my identity to be wrapped up in sports. He knew I had a strong personality as I'd always be talking and trying to goof off. He knew how to talk to me while not breaking my spirit; every day it was fun going to his class.

Another mentor was George Kinnerly, my basketball coach when I was in grades 7 and 9. He was a different mentor than I had been used to as he set parameters more strongly, which was what I needed at those impressionable ages. Basketball was my first love and he once kicked me off the basketball team for one game. As I sat in the stands, I realized how much I missed playing and vowed to play by his rules. I just played football then because it was another sport and I was a good athlete, so it came easy to me.

He was the first person to really instill the work ethic in me that I have today. But, I used to complain because I didn't think all that work was necessary. We had the best athletes in the city and a great team and he would rather run us and discipline us than let us play basketball. Coach Kinnerly wanted me to develop good skills and be conscious of establishing good work habits. He also showed me that my personal behavior was important regardless of my athletic ability.

By grade 9 I accepted what he had taught me and that's when we really started developing my basketball skills and preparing me for my high school years. He pushed me, but it wasn't so much of a push as me making a decision to embrace the knowledge he was sharing. He used to drive me home from practice and always made sure I knew my academic work was just as important. I think he was the first coach to tell me I could be a great player. I understood that he believed in me and he spent a lot of time with me to make sure I was conscientious.

Another mentor was my high school football coach, Bill Conley, who is an Assistant Coach at Ohio State. He took over in grade 11 as I was getting ready to stop playing football and concentrate on basketball. At that time, Butch was in his second year in the NBA. I loved basketball, so that was an instant dream of mine and I almost followed him. I was getting ready to quit football and then they hired Coach Conley. I was the first player he met. He sat me down and asked me if I wanted to be All-American, the team for which the best high school players across the country are selected to play. Well, I was pretty stunned and said 'of course.' He assured me that if I worked hard, he could promise me I'd be an All-American. That blew me away.

But that summer, before the season started, my buddies and I got into trouble with breaking glass in public and I had a scare. Coach Conley brought me into his office and made me understand he would not tolerate that kind of behavior and after that he didn't have any more problems with me. He didn't care how good a football player I was. I had a great junior year and it was the first time I considered that I might play football in college rather than basketball.

I started to get a lot of attention in my senior year. All of the big teams were coming to watch me play and he knew I was dealing with a sensitive subject of whether to choose football or basketball. So, we picked five schools for each sport that were recruiting me and then narrowed it down to one in each; for basketball, The University of Louisville; and Ohio State for football. Coach Conley helped in my decision-making process to choose football as my career.

I didn't know at the time that he was preparing me for college football, not just to get by at the high school level. He believed in hard work and worked me as I'd never been worked before in my life. But, he also gave me tremendous confidence. And yes, I became All–American after my senior year.

The confidence and work ethic these men and other mentors instilled in me is long-lasting. They did not tell me what I wanted to hear; they told me what I needed to hear at the points in my life that I was receptive. Joe Torre, now manager of the New York Yankees was the youngest of five children. Like me, his concept of leadership and mentorship was shaped early by his siblings. His older brother Frank was a baseball player, as Joe would later become. While consciously going to seek out a mentor is a positive step, don't ignore the mentors within your family.

Sometimes you purposefully start developing a mentor relationship, often it's only later in life that you realize their true influence and importance.

"A human being is happiest and most successful when dedicated to a cause outside his own individual, selfish satisfaction."

BENJAMIN SPOCK (PEDIATRICIAN & AUTHOR)

WHO ARE YOUR MENTORS?
WHAT ARE THE THREE BEST THINGS YOU HAVE
LEARNED FROM EACH?
DO THEY KNOW THEY MADE AN IMPRINT ON YOUR LIFE?
CAN YOU PASS THEIR LESSONS ON TO OTHERS?

Money

My son asked me where we get our money from and when I told him I get paid for playing football, he was shocked, saying, "You mean they pay you all that money to play football?" No kidding, because I do play the game for the love of it.

I'm a firm believer that having money doesn't change the person inside, it just makes you more of whomever you are. If you're an essentially good person, you'll still be a good person with money, but if you are essentially a jerk, you'll likely be a bigger jerk. If you have little money, obviously you have constraints and pressures, but who you are as a person does not change. What money does is give you a tremendous opportunity to support your life, to go places and live how you want. It allows you to do things you've just dreamed of, especially in providing opportunities for your children.

People always think they deserve money, but no one throws down a million dollars on a table in front of you and then walks away. You have to work for your money. I believe that certain people have earned the right to compensation. Through my hard work and my talent, I've earned the right to have the resources that I have now, but I didn't deserve money just because I wanted it.

Those in football and other professional sports have picked a profession where there is only a few who will land the big contracts. I'm not saying my profession is as valuable on the world stage as that of a teacher, but a profession such as a teacher is somewhat an easier route in developing a career based on a progression and longevity. And, hopefully teachers don't get banged around a lot. Football is a highly physical contact sport and few make it to the pinnacle.

If tell a boy to follow his heart, as I say to kids all the time, the chances are slim – one in a million – that the boy will end up with a professional contract at the end of school. Although I don't want to take away his dream, it's a big commitment and just plain hard work. Some just will never have what it takes. The saying that "broad is the path but narrow is the gate" is true. It's the survival of the fittest. A lot of people I grew up with had athletic ability, but that is just one part of a person, along with mental and social preparation.

A hard part about having money at a young age is that if you look at the make-up of the backgrounds, a lot of athletes don't come from families that have had a lot of resources. A disadvantaged child's outlook on money is skewed because they may not have grown up around people who had money or have saved money. Therefore, they don't know how to handle it. They don't see it in use. They don't see the good it can do and the daily distress it removes. They are used to living from paycheck to paycheck. This was certainly the case in my family, because we didn't have a lot of money, me being the second last of seven children brought up by a single mother.

When kids of any income bracket are not taught what a bank account is for, how to save money from a part-time job, or how to spend money wisely, it snowballs into an adult not knowing how to balance a checkbook, understand credit card charges or amortize a mortgage.

Our mother showed us how to work hard and said it would pay off, but we were not taught how to handle money because we didn't have any. Nothing could prepare me for what was going to happen when I signed my first NFL contract. I made a lot of mistakes in the early years and was blowing money to buy things I didn't need. We also think we can buy people's love and we make tremendous mistakes before we realize we can sometimes hinder people if we help financially.

It's a good idea to put yourself on a budget and live within the resources you have. You can't drive a $40,000 car if you're making $20,000 a year. You just can't buy a million-dollar house if you're making $100,000 a year. It's important to manage your assets and get help if you need it.

I've always had representation with the agent, Mitch Frankel, who's done a tremendous job of keeping me focused. He kept me on track and educated me. This is especially important for young people as they need someone they can trust to educate them on resources, how to handle wealth and about planning for a secure financial future. I'm now involved with the business world and have gradually begun to make investments. I began to learn about investments, return on money and the risk on return. Although I liked numbers and math in high school, I never had to sit down and understand all of that detail before.

I see so many people who just blow their resources. It's difficult in football as you may have a contract, which is a good and a bad thing. You think you're guaranteed some big sum and then it's hard to plan. You head off to buy cars for everyone in your family because you want to be generous, take care of them or make something up to them. But as soon as you go into the pros, everyone thinks you have money so if you make financial commitments, it creates a lot of long-term debt. You think you're going to play for 10 years and end up playing only two. While great contracts give you a head start on opportunities ahead of some of the people you went to college with, in sports there's no crystal ball that says you're going to have a long career. Then you're out of a job while still being financial indebted.

You have to parlay your resources to allow you to have a future. This can be hard to do as a lot of the players think they are born to play football and that's not the truth. They have to realize there's more to life and sometimes it causes a tremendous identity crisis. Additional jobs are hard to keep because they're hard to balance in the off-season and a player has to keep up with the guys who are training and keep focused. And, toward the end of any career is normally when people are going to make the most money as they've developed an expertise and experience.

With my 14th season coming up, I feel lucky as well as proud of my hard work. With an average of four years for players in the NFL and people now switching jobs so frequently, it's important to get a plan in place to help you, no matter what profession you practice. As a young player, it's hard to visualize that three years might be all that you can play, especially if pro sports has been your goal since you were a teenager. If I had not been playing as long as I have been, I would have some serious financial issues.

There's nothing wrong if you want to sell used cars if that's what you want to do in life, but one thing players have to get over is the need for attention. Very few people have the visibility they did in their sports life; they don't get the VIP treatment they are used to, the free meals or free rounds on the golf courses. That's hard for some former sports stars to make that adjustment. That's another important reason to take care of your assets early and plan, whether you want a financially-fulfilling career or to simplify your life and downscale your high profile job to provide you with a financial cushion.

"Money can't buy friends, but you can get a better class of enemy."

SPIKE MILLIGAN (COMEDIAN & AUTHOR)

ARE YOU EQUATING YOUR VALUES WITH MONEY?
INSTEAD OF MAKING MORE MONEY, CAN YOU LIVE ON LESS?
DOES TRYING TO MAKE MONEY COMPROMISE YOUR
LIFE BALANCE?
DO YOU WANT MONEY TO MAKE YOU FEEL BETTER, WHEN
THERE IS SOMETHING ELSE YOU SHOULD BE DOING FOR
YOUR SOUL?

"Since Christ himself has passed through the test of suffering He is able to help those who are meeting their test now."

HEB 2:18 (A CHRISTIAN'S PRAYER BOOK)

My Relationship with God

When people question why God would allow war and strife, but care about me scoring a touchdown, they are missing the point of His teachings. God is concerned about the things we are concerned with; He can be concerned about individual people and also be concerned about larger life issues. If you look at what's going on in the world, it reflects what's going on in the Bible. There has always been war and there will always be war; this is not anything new. Although we may not always understand the significance of an event, we need to understand there are reasons; such as a simplistic view that if World War II had not taken place, we would not be living in the largely free world we have now.

Likewise, some people believe that they can pray to God for what they wish, but fail to realize only God decides if it will be fulfilled. If not, a person might be praying as a form of escapism rather than a true belief in God's plan. Belief in God and practicing a religion is not a crutch to prop you up when times are tough, it's a way of life and a belief system that is your rock-solid foundation throughout life.

We have to realize there is always going to be suffering and distress. We have to have faith God knows what's best. I well know it's a hard thing in accepting God's will. But, I believe that all things do work for our good. At the time they are occurring, we can't see that bad things are potentially working for our good, but it does work for our betterment in the overall scheme of things. One way to help out is by assuming some of the burden of other people by a simple kind phrase, a helping hand, compassion and support. In our own unique ways, it's our individual responsibility to bear some of the burdens of others and our communities.

If you are a foster parent or adopting abandoned children, donating money or being a volunteer – these are all ways you can ease suffering. Some friends of mine have just adopted a baby girl from China – a country that promotes one child per family with an unfortunate cultural preference for a male child. What I see through this adoption of one single person is saving this innocent child from a difficult life, and knowing that a positive ripple effect is being created around her life and that of her new family. While it's unfortunate our friends cannot have a biological child, they have taken a painful situation and created much good.

Talents – whether athletic, artistic or creative – are a gift from God and what you do and how you live your life is reflecting the thanks and appreciation back to Him. I know that I can use my athletic talent to fulfill God's purpose in my life, as God is not opposed to gains that you make from your gifts. Our unique gifts are not so much to bring glory to us as they are to bring glory to God. I want Him to reap the benefits, whether it is the way I raise my children or that I do well at my job – it's the same God.

I remember a caller to a radio show saying that when I raised my hand to the sky when I scored a touchdown, I was raising my hand to taunt the defenders. That action had and has nothing to do with what's happening on the field – it is an open statement of thanks and humility that I recognize God in my life and I am thanking Him. When I drop down to my knees I offer thanks and say a short prayer as part of my relationship with God.

However, this public action of raising my arm also has two other objectives: it is a testimony to others that they can express their faith without people talking down to them or with a fear of persecution. It also brings believers to me and provides an opportunity to tell my story. It allows me to be a witness of great glory and gives me a chance to be in a state of humility before the Lord. The honor makes me realize it's not me and my ability that I'm reflecting, it's my God-given ability for which I am thankful. I know God is concerned that I am doing what He told me to do. People don't realize that I am trying to take attention from myself and reflect it back to Him in appreciation.

In the 98/99 season, the Minnesota Vikings were one game away from going to the Super Bowl and I thanked God for the opportunity to participate. I never asked God if we were going to the Super Bowl. I thought I was operating in faith by going with it all. I just assumed since He gave us the best season, that was His will and I prayed to be used for His glory, to be healthy and go to the playoffs. When we lost that game, I prayed with and for the Atlanta Falcons so they could realize God's gift and take advantage of that once-in-a-lifetime opportunity and see it as the embodiment of their talents; to not take the experience for granted.

Now, some might ask me that if God really cared about me going to the Super Bowl, couldn't I basically have an easy ride and walk through the challenges like Moses and the parting of the Red Sea? If it's God's destiny for you, why sweat? Because that is taking a faulty argument and not connecting it to what I wrote earlier, in that often we don't know the reasons for His actions or the significance of events. Besides, you can't have 50 players on 12 different teams all thinking they are chosen by God to be in the Super Bowl. But, what we can do is use our God-given talents to express our appreciation for His gift of the opportunity.

I believe I am going to Super Bowl in my career – given what

I know about my purpose in life. This is not something I would be so bold as to say God has shown to me – this is a pure desire of my heart as a human being, as a man and, of course, as a professional football player. I have human goals and one of my personal goals is reach the ultimate dream of playing and winning the Super Bowl. You can be as spiritual as you want to, but you have human needs and must earn money and eat food for the sustenance of your flesh or you'll die.

God is my source – the source is not a single man, not my job and not even my spouse. This helps keep me balanced and helps me to be humble. It helps me with my relationship with my children. I also believe that if God wants me somewhere else He opens a door. God brings a magnifying glass into your life and allows you to reveal and to know what is the right way for you. You can put out your fears and talk to Him. I was called to be a minister because of this strong belief. I wanted to be able to translate my understanding of God to others. I wanted someone to ask me a question and be able to give back a greater understanding of who God is and His importance.

In my ministry I try to be as simple as possible and relate the word of Jesus Christ to modern life and make the teachings relevant. Jesus was simple and related to everyday activities of peoples' lives and that's what I try to do. Agriculture was then the most widespread and laborious of service so Jesus spoke to people in language they could understand. He spoke to them in parables of the soil and the sky and the sun and related it to their lives. The ministry of Jesus was to meet people where they lived without judgement and it's simply hard to rediscover these messages in today's turbulent world. God has allowed me to experience different things in my life and given the depth of my suffering, I have a greater understanding and empathy for people in all walks of life.

For those who have not found God in their lives, but are interested in learning more, I encourage people to seek God's guidance. If you seek and accept God, the messages will provide opportunities for you to change your life. When a person has reached a low point, they talk to friends or they may pray, almost unaware that is what they are doing. Even if they don't have a belief in God, they say something such as "please God, help me through this." Often this comes literally on a person's deathbed, when they ask God for help. So, of course, I encourage people to discover God now so they can experience the peace of God throughout life.

I also encourage people to find a church where there is a Bible class and to read the Bible daily, although it can be overwhelming at first. It is the greatest story ever written. Not understanding the Bible is an excuse – you have to make yourself available to be taught. If you're 35 years old and you now want God in your life, you really are a toddler in Christ and no one can teach you if you're not receptive to the messages.

The learning and understanding is an ongoing process. If you can read books on how to understand the way you think and are in search of comprehension, you can find fulfillment. Those who have been believers for years know that God reveals more the deeper the walk, as there is so much in the Bible to learn. I don't think the way I thought five years ago, and as I continue to learn and explain, my faith continues to deepen my understanding.

"Find the good. It's all around you. Find it, showcase it and you will start believing it."

JESSE OWENS (ATHLETE)

WHAT GIVES YOU SPIRITUAL FULFILLMENT?
TO WHOM DO YOU OWE YOUR SUCCESSES?
HOW WILL YOU LEARN ABOUT WHAT YOU NEED
TO UNDERSTAND?
ARE YOU USING PAST EXPERIENCES IN YOUR LIFE
(GOOD & BAD) FOR THE BETTERMENT OF OTHERS?
WHAT IS YOUR PURPOSE IN LIFE?

Racism

When you are black in a relatively white part of the world, you are never invisible. You can never be anonymous. You can rarely be just one of the crowd. Somehow you always stick out; whether shopping in a store that appears beyond your means, in a lineup at an airport when you are pulled over to be searched, or even engaged in the most benign pursuit of leisure; taking a walk in a park. Maybe not in your own neighborhood if the people are predominantly of one race, but in the United States as a whole, you stick out.

The ways people express racism can be seemingly soft and innocuous, such as when I walk onto the elevator and a woman grabs her purse, or when a driver reaches over and locks his doors when I drive up beside him at a traffic light. I was visiting a new city once and was looking for a gym that I knew was close by. I saw a man with a window rolled down and I went up to ask directions. He just turned and looked straight ahead, ignoring me.

These are not fanciful notions of my imagination. There is plenty of indirect racism. My wife always shops at the same grocery store, and when my brother came to town he went to get the groceries that night, and paid with a $100 bill. The cashier checked the bill with a counterfeit pencil and it was fine. She then went to get the manager, and the two of them went into the manager's back office where they both checked the bill. Now, this is a place we always shop and they have never asked us questions or checked our money.

I've been at the airport wearing a t-shirt and sweats like many other men and a woman asked me if I was for hire, or some woman thinks she's being original by telling me I should be an athlete. I've had salespeople come to the door of my home and tell me to go get the owner of the house. If I'm sitting in first class on a plane, the flight attendant might say that a man in front wants a soda, and the other will ask what I look like or where I'm sitting. Most often, I'm described as the black man. I also shake my head at crime reports on the radio, because if the suspect is black, it's the first thing that's reported.

It's hurtful to know that when my wife is in a store she is being followed by security and once, being told by the manager she fit the profile of a shoplifter. My wife used to work in retail and points out that if the security guard had been observant – he would have noticed her jewelry or clothing instead of her skin color. It's distressing to watch her being passed over to be served because another shopper looks like they can better afford what's in the display case.

In playing football, I have often heard the word "nigger" used against visiting players by the fans of the hometown team. If they are yelling at me, I try to get them to calm down by asking them, 'What would you call me if I played for your team?' I've only heard a white player use it once during a practice. African-American players may use the n-word among them but it doesn't mean the same thing or have the same connotation because it's used like "brother-man." Another expression of racism is when

I'm dressed up after a game speaking to reporters and someone tells me that I speak so nicely, as if that's so unusual for a black man and I should be gratified to be praised. I don't hear anyone condescendingly telling my white teammates that they speak well, although I'm sure white players have been insulted also, on and off the field. An example of this stigma is in white players being told they can't perform in certain skilled positions, but that is true for blacks also. There are very few white receivers just as there are very few black quarterbacks.

Sports is a great integrator of the races; it forces people to play on the same teams with people of different backgrounds. Even so, there is an automatic separation of the races in the NFL. It is unspoken, but it exists. When I go to the cafeteria, I'll try to go out of my way to sit with the white players on occasion. I don't have to, but I choose to both to break my consciousness and theirs.

With three-quarters of the NFL players being black, there is integration, but we all still need a reminder to create change. I find it stunning that only two of the 31 head coaches are black. It seems we're good enough to play the game, but not good enough to coach. This goes back to conscious thought in the owners and managers giving people opportunities, such as being a Division 1 college coach or an offensive/defensive coordinator in the NFL and moving on up. But surprisingly, many black coaches are not even given an interview for head coaching positions. (Many books examine the issues and you may want to start with *A Hard Road to Glory: the African-American Athlete in Football*, by tennis groundbreaker Arthur Ashe. Part of a series on blacks in sports, the book is a wonderful compendium of statistics, anecdotes, facts and reasoning that grew from a seminar he gave in 1981 on the historical and sociological roles of black athletes.)

With our children, we have never referred to people as black or white, because we don't want to draw attention to skin color as if it should be a consideration. When our family first moved into one community, my son asked us how all the brown women could have white babies – noting of course the overwhelming prevalence of black nannies caring for white children. Our babysitter, who is of Italian heritage, receives many stares and actual comments when she is out in public caring for our children. Even in our own communities, my wife is fearful of driving at night through the city and stopping in the dark because of the experience of others – and ourselves one day – of the actions of some police officers.

Many years ago, I was driving with Melanie in my new car when I was in playing with the Philadelphia Eagles. It was a miserable day. There was a wild snowstorm and we were crossing a bridge with a high wind blowing. I was pulled over by a police officer for speeding. I knew I had not been, and pointed out to the officer that there was no possible way I could have been speeding with the snowstorm and treacherous bridge crossing in the wind. Besides, I was being extra cautious that day as I was driving my brand new car.

Within a few minutes, the police officer recognized me and apologized for pulling me over before wishing me well on my way. He knew my name and my profession, and that indeed I could be the owner of the car. The fact that I was a young black man driving a brand new Mercedes was not lost on me, as traditionally we have not been in financial situations to afford such luxury. The sad thing is this is still happening today in North America, which just perpetuates the disparity.

Our family lives in a predominately white society and community. Our son asks us how come there are not more black people with homes like ours. We understand that blacks have not held much economic power in North America and it will unfortunately take many more years of true acceptance into established settings. But, it is far too slow a process of genuine acceptance.

At a country club in New Albany, Chicago, my family was enjoying the swimming pool, when a boy of some six years old asked me "how did you get here from Africa?" It irritated me that he was being taught some old model as I knew he didn't come out with that on his own. Initially, I said he should just tell his parents we were Black-Americans. But later I just felt sorry for the kid, because if that is what his parents think, he's going to miss out on a lot of richness in life. At least he didn't scramble out of the pool when we came in, which has happened.

I didn't experience a lot of racism as a youth because of my athletic involvement. Many times I didn't have transportation to the practice or games and many white parents of friends of mine would pick me up or give me rides home. I had heard about people being afraid of coming into my neighborhood, but most had no problem. You have to remember, I grew up in a very poor urban area and I looked at people differently. I treated a person how they treated me – even though I knew about racism – I gave people the benefit of the doubt. If they treated me fairly from a very young age that was good. I am not naive, as I do know direct racism is out there. But, in my experience it has been limited as to the bluntness.

At one time, my daughter and son were the only blacks in their school and I asked my son how he felt about it. He said, with a resigned old wisdom – when he was only six years old – that it didn't matter to him as he had always been the only black kid. I thought of my grandmother being the first black to graduate from her high school all those decades ago and realized nothing much had changed.

As far as providing opportunities for my daughter and son to be among black culture, the church we go to is predominately black and we have a loving extended family. I am glad our children have not had the experiences – yet – of direct racism, although the indirect racism is cruel. I know the time will come. We are raising them to know fully that one person doesn't speak for a whole race. This concept is important to communicate to all. In July 1999, Colin Powell talked of his church adopting an inner-city school and poignantly, one of the children said he now knew that old white men were not enemies; as how could they be enemies since one such man spent every Saturday morning tutoring him?

There is not only racism from whites to be concerned with – there may be discrimination by other races, kids who were not raised with the benefits my children have had, or from other blacks. Intra-cultural racism exists among blacks with the sentiment of pitting blacks against each other depending on their "blackness." It's a sad statement that we are compelled to describe ourselves with a preface as saying we are Black-American or African-American, as if saying just 'American' isn't enough. Some say the double label honors the African heritage, but others say its just another label.

I feel it takes the same amount of energy for people to teach racism and ignorance, as it takes to teach acceptance and respect. I just hope the children of this generation have a better chance for acceptance and respect than the generation in which we were raised.

"Racism is a contempt for life, an arrogant assertion that one race is the center of value and object of devotion, before which other races must kneel in submission."

MARTIN LUTHER KING JR. (CLERIC, CIVIL RIGHTS LEADER & AUTHOR)

DO YOU SEE DIRECT OR INDIRECT RACISM?
WHAT HAVE YOU BEEN TAUGHT?
ARE YOU AWARE OF ANY RACIST THOUGHTS OR ACTIONS?
WHO ARE YOUR FRIENDS IN YOUR SOCIAL CIRCLE: ARE THEY INCLUSIVE OF OTHER RACES?

"You are ultimately responsible for you. You must not expect anyone else to take care of you. If they do, fine, but don't rely on anyone else other than you and God for your self-survival. Never let anyone take your independence away."

KATHY RUSSELL (AUTHOR)

Self-Discipline

We've all done it. Woken up late on a cold rainy Saturday morning, maybe after staying out late the night before. All you want to do is roll over and settle back into that warm bed and dream, but you suddenly remember you have to get to practice or have to get to all those house chores you promised you'd do. So, you make a little deal with yourself that you'll wait until the clock hits a quarter past; then you'll get up. Then another quarter hour, then it's too late to get moving.

Whoever invented the snooze button on clock radios must have been a procrastinator at heart, because that little button is an annoying – but helpful – reminder that you need to actually use some self-discipline to put your feet to the floor. It's easy to have great self-discipline on the things you want to do – but the measure of a person is when you try to accomplish the things you don't want to do. To me, self-discipline is not doing what you want to do, but doing what you should do or what you dislike doing, but see that there's a reason.

Whether you have homework, a project hanging over your head or put off getting on that treadmill for another day, you're just hurting yourself in the long run. With self-discipline and setting goals, you are taking baby steps every day that add up to something important. The ability to start a project and finish it shows you how to deal with frustration, how to overcome procrastination and gives you a unequaled sense of personal accomplishment. This is true whether you are completing a night class, trying to lose 20 pounds or overcoming an addiction.

I shouldn't admit it, but I don't want to work out – I really don't. It's hard to be disciplined for a long time doing the same things and I've been working out almost daily since I can remember. It's become a routine. The main thing is, I understand that working out is part of my job even though I don't like it. Have I missed a practice because of laziness? Yes. Have I been in bed an extra hour because I just didn't want to get up? Of course. For me, I have a hard time doing something if there is no goal. Part of me is like the kid who asks his mom just why he needs to do something. A kid can't always equate success and failure to his or her own actions. I believe I do have great self-discipline now and I realize the benefits.

I have plenty of struggles – do I call in, work out, take the day off – all those things are going on in my mind the same as everyone, but my discipline is what keeps me going. Of course you could say I'm being paid a lot of money to work out, but the fact is, it still takes self-discipline. I wish that every year I could show up for training camp and be in great shape and get great results. But, I love being on the field and realize it's all related, so I can deal with the pain and agony of working out at 6 in the morning off-season or on. It's easy to get fired up if there's 60,000 people watching and a huge television audience.

Some people in the NFL are not disciplined, which just reflects the general population, really. Some always go through life without self-discipline or in living for the moment, unconcerned with long-term effects or their personal responsibility. They might tend to procrastinate and put things off, or somehow always forget. But, it all boils down to self-discipline and actual self-respect so that you can accomplish your unique goals.

One method I find helps me be disciplined is by setting goals. Otherwise, I'm floundering. So, I see self-discipline and goals tied together to get my best results. Since I was in high school, I have always set short term, medium and long range goals. In fact, my goals from high school still drive me today and I'm very goal-oriented as far as my profession, marriage and our children. I'm always setting small goals to improve what I do.

It may sound strange, but it's easier to reach your goals if you work on your weaknesses rather than your strengths. To be a complete football player, parent or student, you have to work on the things you don't do very well. For example; as a football player I have to work on being faster. If you work on your strengths, it doesn't make you better overall, it just makes your strengths more pronounced. While it's good to be able to master a task or attribute, pay attention to your weaknesses and improve the whole "you."

For an example of this, I look at a player such as Joe Montana, who was a good player at Notre Dame, but it took him a long time to get to play because he was smaller than average. Few thought he'd be the great quarterback he was in San Francisco, but he worked hard to make himself a great player and what he needed to work on. This relates to how people can turn their weaknesses into assets and I talk to young people all the time about that. It's the same with Vince Carter of the Toronto Raptors. If he continued to just work on his jumping ability and slam dunks, he's only going to be so good. But he's working in other areas now and he's just at the beginning of a great career.

Everyone has weaknesses; it's just a matter of how those weaknesses are handled. With me, being a man and a father, I feel I have weaknesses I have to work on every day. Except for my mother's parents, I didn't grow up around great long-lasting marriages, so I didn't have a lot of role models in how to be a great husband. Even when you set goals, it's easy to get sidetracked, so give yourself mini-goals; give yourself something to shoot at that's achievable. One of the tricks I use is to just start something for five minutes. By the time that five minutes is over, I'm usually so into the task at hand that I want to keep going.

This also relates to other peoples' checks and balances, as then you don't always have to have them correcting you or reminding you; maybe waiting in the background terrified (or happy!) you might fail. If you set goals and accomplish them through self-discipline, then you would be able to achieve more for yourself and be responsible. And don't set your goals too low just so you can say you've accomplished what you set out to do!

Like many people, I tend to make excuses and procrastinate. For example, I wish I read more, but I start a book, and then someone gives me something that is far more important or interesting to read, so I pick that one up. While I have become better because of self-discipline, it's also human to be a bit unfocused. Now that I realize I'm a procrastinator, I don't take on more than I can handle. Being realistic about yourself and your habits will always test your self-discipline, as sometimes you actually need to know when you can relax about something. Ultimately though, for the bigger things in life, to be a happy person you must be productive and to be productive you must be disciplined.

"There is no such thing as freedom without discipline. The one who is free is disciplined"

JANET COLLINS (DANCER)

DO YOU TEND TO RESPECT YOURSELF AND YOUR GOALS BY BEING SELF-DISCIPLINED?
DO YOU EVER "SHOOT YOURSELF IN THE FOOT" BY SPECIFICALLY NOT DOING THINGS YOU SHOULD?
WHAT EFFECT DOES THIS BEHAVIOR HAVE?

What Having Children Brings to Your Life

Many parents say that having children brings balance to their lives, but what I think they really mean is that having kids means not being able to be selfish. That means everything from putting your children as the priority, moving towns where your children might thrive better – as my Mom moved our family when we were young – and simple things like doing crafts with them when you'd really rather be watching television.

It also means being more conscious in knowing that time truly is precious and moves fast. My wife and I have a son and a daughter, and as I've gotten older, I've started to understand the time we spend together now is invaluable. And, not just for me – for all of us. Any parent will also tell you that kids grow up before your eyes; and you might think that's simplistic or laugh it off, but I want to retain a sense of my children and their innocence as long as possible.

Our kids bring me a sense of reward, a treasure every day and they make every ache and pain from football or practice worthwhile. When I'm tired after a game they can jump on me and rough me up and it soothes me. There was never so gentle a touch as my son or daughter's hand on my arm or a sweeter sound than one of them calling "Daddy" out to me. I feel so proud that I am able to provide for them and give them a lifestyle even better than in my dreams – in compensation I suppose from my childhood.

Although my brothers and sisters and I had good values instilled in us growing up, there was no money. Being able to provide for your children honestly and without spoiling them is an honor. When I was young, I couldn't help but look out over the basketball court or football field and imagine a better day when I could afford to do what I wanted, buy the clothes I desired or go where I wanted. Watching television and seeing sports events couldn't help but open up a whole new world and I wanted a part of it. But, the best thing about being able to provide for my family in doing what I want to do, is to have potential and possibilities open to them. Plus, we also really cherish the simple things that being in a family allows, such as going to church, eating meals together, working on projects and reading.

I try to do simple things like taking them to school and picking them up, and I try to do most of the errands I need to do when they're in school. I'm also the early bird in our home. They enjoy me cooking breakfast for them and I try to do a lot of little things like that. It's easy for me to get them breakfast and I enjoy going upstairs to wake them up. This way, the time I am with them, I am really with them. They realize football is what I do for my job but I don't make it out to be a big deal because when I'm with them, I just want to be their Dad. This role as father also keeps me grounded when I've had professional success – so that's part of the balance my children bring me.

I also enjoy the things I can do for them to make them feel

special as people in learning about social behavior and their role in the world. I enjoy watching them grow and develop friendships and having them invite friends over to visit.

Our guidance as parents comes through conversation, our belief in God and having good values. It's important for them to see me do the same things I tell them. I get involved in what they're involved in. So many parents make the mistake of steering children in a different direction than the direction in which the kids are interested. If my kids are not interested in a particular job, why would I want them to be miserable human "doings" instead of human beings and waste their individual gifts and talents? There are too many people already in jobs they hate.

For me, I loved the competition aspect of sports. If I let Duron only play football and he decides to play tennis, then my involvement in his sports life may be limited based on my understanding. If he wants to play basketball, I'm not going to steer him away from it. I've had a good life in sports and know the value of sports in a child's life, such as teamwork, achievement and discipline. But, whatever my kids want to do – to me it would not matter – they should still largely do what they want to express their unique talents and gifts.

As parents, teachers and coaches, we are here to nurture and develop children. We are not here to make all the decisions for kids. I enjoy knowing I can provide opportunities for my children, but our biggest role is that in being parents and leaders, we are supposed to be helping them gain the skills and thought processes so they can make the right decisions to help them throughout their lives.

Kids also have a way of getting to the core of your heart and taking you down a notch. At the game, whether I've won or lost, Duron will ask, "Well Dad, why didn't you catch that ball?" I just have to laugh, but if it was anybody else, maybe I'd not be so accepting. I also see a lot of myself in my children and especially in Monterae's personality. It's easy for a man to see so much in his boys and maybe it's still the "Daddy's girl" scenario because she is young, but she makes me feel as if I'm the strongest, best, most handsome man in the world. She also likes to read and likes to paint, which is very different from Duron, who likes all sports and anything to do with a ball – a Carter family trait it seems – but I think she has my gentle quiet side.

During the season, when I'm covered in ice bags, the kids pray for all my aches and pains. They pray on the way to school for God to bless me and of course there's Monterae saying, "God, please let Daddy get six touchdowns." Well, that also makes me laugh and it gives me an opportunity to talk about the role of God in our lives and how God does not always give us what we want – like parents.

Although I really believe there is a biological difference between boys and girls, how my personality, talents and discipline as a person and a parent becomes reflected in my children continues to amaze me. For example, because I study moves and plays and do a lot of research and homework, both my children have observed this trait and habit in me.

They have now translated this trait into their own lives, with Duron now studying moves and plays and then doing it himself on the ball field. Monterae also loves any kind of dance and watches as much as possible. It fascinates her. She watches dance, figure skating, ballet and is now also into choreography. I believe they got those skills from me because I'm the same way. I have been known to be called graceful in my moves on the field – but I hope Monterae doesn't base her dance moves on my moves! I am so thankful that I can see a good trait in me develop into habits for them; skills which will last their lifetimes.

If you are a young person, I know what your parents say sometimes goes through one ear and out the other and I know all that we might tell you isn't hip or cool or what you want to hear. But, you will know as you reach a certain age or have life experiences and certainly children of your own, that childhood is a wonderfully precious time. We get as much from you as you hopefully get from us and we just hope our stewardship of your life passes on through each generation.

"Children have never been very good at listening to their elders, but they have never failed to imitate them."

JAMES BALDWIN (AUTHOR)

WHETHER YOU HAVE CHILDREN, COUSINS, NIECES OR NEPHEWS, HOW DO CHILDREN ENRICH YOUR LIFE?
HOW DO YOU MAKE LIFE BETTER FOR A CHILD?
HOW DO YOU ENCOURAGE CHILDREN TO DRAW ON THEIR POTENTIAL?
HOW CAN YOU HELP THE CHILDREN CLOSEST TO YOU TO NOT REGRET THE PAST?

"We must always have the three D's: Desire, Dedication and Determination. We must not let anything turn us aside. And to be truly successful, we must always reach back and try to lift someone else as we climb."

HAZEL B. GARLAND (JOURNALIST & EDITOR)

When to be an Individual & When to be a Team Player

There's a fine line between being a strong individual and doing what's good for the team. The pressure on athletes in all stages is tremendous. It's a constant walk between being or appearing selfish and participating as a team member and achieving team goals. But it's done all the time; just look at Magic Johnson, who is a great athlete and plays the game with flair, but had a way of playing that made everyone around him better.

When people say the 80's decade was the "me" decade, the detractors and "me-decade people" did a disservice to the greater ideals of collaboration and harmony. When people were out pursuing their own goals at all costs, many forgot the effect on their family, their community and their colleagues. This notion of individual pursuit at any cost disparaged the idea that we are put on this planet to live in concert with other people, not just playing our own tune. Whether you are in sports or business or working on a class project with others, these are situations that all help to define your role as an individual in a team environment.

Learning about how the dynamics of your role can affect the team is a life-long process and you must intrinsically know when to step forward to shine and when to step back to let others shine. So much of the game is in the strategy, the homework, your own personal preparation and your thinking. Then, when you get into the flow of the game, things change and you don't do what you've been anticipating. You're not rehearsing anymore. That's over and now it's time to do what you were trying to do all week. And, you have to remember the other team is being paid a lot of money and has had the same practice and is preparing to stop you from doing what you intend.

If I go into a football game one week and have to match up with a certain defensive back, during the first half I may have caught one pass that's admired. But if I'm in the game a lot and someone says I'm selfish, that I've been in the game too long, or the quarterback throws to me, they may not know that was the game plan. There are certain weeks it's been part of the game plan that I am supposed to be playing a big part of the game. Some weeks I'll be the decoy. Some weeks I'll be the main player. Besides being part of the game plan, opportunity presents itself to you and that balance of knowing when to perform or hang back and let others shine, is something you do learn as you get older. If you have to climb on the backs of others to elevate yourself rather than bringing others up with you, you are not a team player.

Football is different from most other sports, because there's a designed play for every situation. What I do is try to concentrate on every play – even if I'm not the receiver – in case the running back breaks free. Then the running back can get the glory and I'm just thinking about doing my job. The quarterback can be a bit more dangerous or conservative; he's in that position where he can make that distinction, where he can really be selfish and that's expected.

We are working as a team in unison but a lot of talented individuals are doing their job to make up the team and sometimes some are greater than others – sometimes you have to step up as an individual and sometimes come together as a team. But it does come back to being selfless. The more you can be selfless, the better team player you can be, while still realizing you are going to reach your goals. That's easier for me now as most of my goals are wrapped up into the team's goals. When I was younger, I was more wrapped up in my individual goals.

When you look at some of the plays of basketball star Michael Jordan, he often hung back and passed to a teammate and allowed other players to make the big shot. That's an especially hard immediate decision to make when it comes at the end of the game. If you're in a good position, do you take a tough long shot or pass to someone in a great position with a good shot? It's hard to be both an individual and a team player when so much of our reward system, appreciation and financial payoff is based on individual achievements. This is especially true for decisions made in a nanosecond when the game's on the line.

If you could have your way you'd be a great player on a great team. If you have a tremendous year, your memories are based on you playing well. I've had great individual accomplishments that fulfill a part of me, but I think the great team accomplishments are longer lasting because the memories are totally different. The wonderful thing is you have memories of other people's achievements, which is rewarding to be part of; the fact that you can help someone also achieve their goals is very fulfilling. It reinforces why you are on a team and the simple fact is if you have a lot of people doing their job well, it allows you do your work better.

I realized I had to depend on a lot of people, and I really expected the most out of them. One thing I've learned is people want to do well but they are often not capable of doing better than they are doing. Certain people have reached their potential – they are not going to reach any higher now. Every person is different, and you can't approach people the same way. So now I'm more tactful and take the make-up and the ability of the person into consideration.

Every athlete thinks they are better than they are. When you're a star player working on a bad team, you wonder if people are going to recognize your achievements the same way they recognize others on good teams. Given the situation they are in, they are probably not even thinking about winning the championship so it may be hard to stay motivated, but that's when you need to also concentrate on doing your best for the sake of the team.

Although you many learn teamwork at a young age, maybe on a high school team or school project, it becomes more difficult as you play with better players or work with highly talented superstars as you might have to sacrifice some of your personal goals for the team. What helps is that is by putting yourself in these situations, you develop a realistic attitude and confidence in yourself and the ability of others. As an athlete, you see tremendous monetary advantages to individual accomplishments.

When we draft a player like Randy Moss, a lot of my individual goals have to be put on the back burner. I didn't know how he would fit with the team. But, I was confident in myself that I would have a lot of opportunities and he wasn't going to take glory away from me. Even if he did, I knew I could handle it and it was fulfilling to me to see him shine and come into his own as a person and talented player. That I have had some effect on encouraging him is professionally and personally rewarding and just reinforces my belief of teamwork. I believe there is enough of the spotlight. I will be a better professional also, but I'm comfortable enough in how I play now in that I know I'll leave my mark.

"Losing doesn't eat at me the way it used to. I just get ready for the next play, the next game, the next season."

TROY AIKMAN (QUARTERBACK, DALLAS COWBOYS)

WHETHER SCHOOL, SPORTS OR BUSINESS, HOW DO YOU BALANCE YOUR INDIVIDUAL GOALS WITH THE GOALS OF YOUR TEAM?

HOW CAN YOU ENCOURAGE OTHER PEOPLE TO SHINE?

ARE YOU COVETOUS OF THE TALENTS OF OTHERS OR CAN YOU COMPLEMENT THEIR SKILLS?

Books I Recommend:

A LESSON BEFORE DYING
BY ERNEST GAINES
A moving story of one man's enforced goal to help an innocent man die with dignity.

THE BLUEST EYE
BY TONI MORRISON
Since its publication in 1970, Morrison's first novel is a poignant account of a persecuted child and the effects of racial and social issues.

DESIGNED BY GOD SO I MUST BE SPECIAL
BY BONNIE SOSE
A collection of poems for young children.

THE GIVING TREE
BY SHEL SILVERSTEIN
A tender children's story of love and self-sacrifice, but there's a great message for people of all ages.

I LOVE YOU AS MUCH
BY LAURA K. MELMED,
HENRI SORENSEN
The comfort of a mother's love through love poems by mother animals to their babies.

LOVE YOU FOREVER
BY ROBERT M. MUNSCH
This gentle tale is bound to make anyone weep with its timeless story of love, aging and role reversal.

SOME SOUL TO KEEP
BY J. CALIFORNIA COOPER
A collection of short stories about strong people, families, dreams and the power of the human spirit.

SOMETHING BEAUTIFUL
BY SHARON DENNIS WYETH
A young girl searches for something beautiful in her harsh neighborhood, finding beauty in people and her community.

TUESDAYS WITH MORRIE
BY MITCH ALBOM
As a tribute to a remarkable teacher, this true story embodies the best of friendship and is told with warmth, empathy and emotion.

Notes

BROTHERS
Born to Believe

Published by Full Wits Publishing Inc.,
Suite 250, Unit 14, 4 Westwood Boulevard,
Upper Tantallon, Nova Scotia, Canada B3Z 1H3.
902-857-1900 tel • 902-857-1771 fax

Full Wits Publishing Inc. gratefully acknowledges the following:

If: Rudyard Kipling North American copyright free. A.P. Wyatt.

I, Too, Sing America: From COLLECTED POEMS by Langston Hughes
Copyright © 1994 by the Estate of Langston Hughes. Reprinted by permission of
Alfred A. Knopf, a Division of Random House Inc.

The full line of fine books from Full Wits Publishing Inc. is available at
select bookstores and direct from the publisher at www.fullwits.com.
For further information, visit our website: **www.fullwits.com**

Canadian Cataloguing in Publication Data

Carter, Butch, 1958-
Born to Believe

Includes 2 separate texts on inverted pages.
Each text has separate cover title reflecting single author.
ISBN 1-894389-05-0

1. Sports — Psychological aspects. 2. Spirituality. 3. Carter, Butch,
1958- 4. Carter, Cris. I. Carter, Cris. II. Martin, Cynthia, 1957-
III. Title.

GV706.55.C37 2000   796'.01   C00-950072-3

Cover photo by: Ron Turenne
Manufactured in Canada by: Print Atlantic
Book layout & design by: Deborah McGowan
First Edition: May 2000

Full Wits Publishing Inc.
www.fullwits.com

BROTHERS
Born to Believe

BY BUTCH CARTER & CRIS CARTER

WITH CYNTHIA MARTIN

personal reflections & inspiration

Full Wits Publishing Inc.
www.fullwits.com

Table of Contents: Butch Carter

*To my mother and the memory of her parents, who
encouraged me to believe in myself. May my lessons and
thoughts continue to provide inspiration to my three cherished
sons, Brandon, Blake and Baron. And to you the reader;
may you know you were born to believe in yourself.*

DEDICATION

Preface & Acknowledgements

Although many athletes write books, I didn't think about it until
I spoke to students at a high school that had been troubled by
racial tension. I was very moved by the reaction of these teenagers
to my words, which you can read about in my chapter on
Community Service. I may not have set the world on fire, but in
my own quiet way, I understand I had simply touched more lives
that day than in coaching any team. And, what I said didn't have
much to do with my life in sports.

I believe so strongly that in giving more attention to their
potential and the decisions they make, young people can
determine their future. In writing my personal views and
incidents from my life in and out of sports, I'm not making
definitive statements about the world. I hope my experiences
will provide some personal encouragement for you. After each
chapter you'll see questions to prompt you and note your own
thoughts, and I urge you to give these consideration. By noting

your personal aspirations, after reading of ordinary men who achieved much in our short lives, my brother Cris and I hope you will believe in the power of your own words and thoughts.

In giving thanks, I really must acknowledge some salient people; first my mother, whom I talk about with love and admiration throughout and my brothers, sisters and their families. I also must thank Glen for giving me an opportunity, Cynthia for her support, patience and guidance, Full Wits Publishing for giving me a chance, Tom for his edits and Stephanie for keeping me organized.

"Each had his past shut in him like the leaves of a book known to him by heart; and his friends could only read the title."

VIRGINIA WOOLF (AUTHOR)

Biography Summary

As the oldest of seven children, Butch Carter was born into a natural life of leading. He was raised predominately by his mother along with three brothers and sisters, including co-author Cris Carter. The family's early years were spent in Midwestern America; Troy and later Middletown, Ohio, where their mother moved them to provide opportunities for her children's involvement in sports and to take a new job to support her family.

A graduate of Indiana University, he was drafted by the Los Angeles Lakers in the 1980 draft, and played seven years of professional basketball in the National Basketball Association (NBA). Butch began coaching in 1986 in Middletown, Ohio. Named 1988 Ohio State Coach of the Year by Associated Press, he is the only person to win both Player of the Year and Coach of the Year honors in the state of Ohio. Moving to the Toronto Raptors in 1997 as assistant coach, then interim coach, he was appointed head coach in June 1998. Butch led the Raptors to their first playoff berth in the 99/00 season, for the first time in Toronto Raptor history. Only two other teams in NBA history have gone from winning less than 20 games to making the playoffs two years later.

With three sons and a large extended family, Butch has retained his appetite for knowledge by keeping extensive notes over the last 22 years on places he has worked and traveled to, and he incorporates the best of his personal experiences in both coaching and parenthood. Part of his success and reputation derives from the fact he cares deeply about providing opportunities for achievement in others and encourages their success.

Basketball has given him the opportunity to travel the world and view the human race's wonderful cultural and ethnic differences.

Introduction

It's no secret that being a father figure and being responsible was the role into which my older brother Butch was born. Growing up in a single parent home was just our script – my brothers and sisters and I didn't know any differently – but we did realize early that Butch largely replaced our father. We turned out to be better people because of this and in overcoming the adversity we faced early in our lives. And, Butch was always there to carry us through whatever problem we were facing as individuals or as a family "team."

Butch's personality always contained a prescient overdose of maturity and mental discipline. He was always an old child with wisdom way beyond his years. Butch has always been a thinker, an observer, a complex character who scanned and filed each experience in his highly intelligent and organized mind. How he came to be a leader is not a mystery. He has always drawn out the best of each person and their potential, while remaining conscious of how that person would fit with others. He has always stressed the positive and tried to eliminate the negative, and he always focused on others, rather than be comfortable with any attention focused on him.

He always had an innate determination that could not be satisfied, I think precisely because everyone had expectations of him, and still do, of being three steps ahead of all of us. That outer reserve people see is his essentially quiet and focused nature that shows how he scans the world and thinks through problems. Rather than getting frustrated or emotional, which would have upset my brothers and sisters, Butch knew from an early age that he had to maintain control and calm leadership for our benefit. Looking to his resolve and the way he dealt with problems was an inspiration to us, although I don't think we appreciated those

attributes when we were children.

While I regret he was thrown into responsibility so young, and did not have the luxury of a childhood that I did as the second youngest child, it is clear he has evolved into a great leader because of this role.

When I was young, he was tough on me although not so tough I'd tune him out. Butch has always allowed me and our brothers and sisters to be kids but more like a father to a son rather than an older brother. In later years, our relationship evolved to brother to brother. He continued to mold me and my strong will, but was careful not to break my spirit.

The issues we talk about in our book are unique and inherently private, but by talking about personal issues, we know people can gain strength from us. For whatever we have achieved good and bad, individually and together, it is always best shared with others.

Cris Carter

"Duke Ellington told me to do two things because you just get burnt out doing one; so I do two. I paint every day."

TONY BENNETT (SINGER & ARTIST)

Addictive Behaviors

Whether it's smoking, taking drugs, working too much or abusing alcohol, many people develop self-destructive behaviors. I've heard many people say they are experimenting or they can stop anytime, but the truth is when you have an addiction, you can often fall back into the problem during times of stress or trouble especially if you lack supports. Once you feel you have one addiction taken care of, you can develop other addictions. Many of these behaviors start out as an experiment, and can end up causing great damage to you, your family, finances, co-workers or friends.

I never was attracted to drugs or abused alcohol. Yet, I know addiction by experience, as I am a workaholic. I started this addictive behavior on Friday nights in high school. I'd turn the lights on in the basketball court because I knew all my teammates would be going to some party and no one would be there to bother me. I could practice to my heart's content.

I made the choice to not go to the parties, and to focus on basketball and what gave me the greatest amount of pleasure. Basketball became my life. Basketball became the focus of every decision outside of school and what was best for me as an athlete. There were some painful nights when my buddies would ride by yelling at me "You're not going to get a girl being on that court," but my goal was to get out of the neighborhood by getting a scholarship. My goal was to get a free education.

This singular focus eventually developed into an obsessive feeling of constantly feeling like I needed to work. That stayed with me through my NBA playing career and into coaching. If I wasn't at work, I'd be close by phone, a cell phone and a pager. This addiction is regrettably still part of me today, although I am trying to break the pattern.

The only time my phones haven't rung off the hooks was the first two months of coaching in Toronto when I took over a team that most considered was the septic tank of the NBA! Even on my birthday, in the off-season, I worked the whole day. The coaching staff was surprised, asking if I was planning on taking the day off or to have a quiet dinner with someone special. I did; I went to dinner with my boss, Glen Grunwald.

This kind of addictive behavior can be as detrimental as substance abuse or any other addiction you can fall into or choose to develop. And many who are workaholics neglect themselves, their families and especially their children in that never-ending quest to gain self-worth in the working world.

For me, I grew up always practicing basketball on Thanksgiving and on Christmas, so you start to devalue those family times. Because you don't eat meals with your family, you also start to spend less time enjoying the natural times of togetherness. You simply can't be stuffing yourself with turkey and then go out and have a productive practice. That just became ingrained as a player – so every Christmas or Thanksgiving I was out practicing or playing a game. I never went out on New Year's Eve because I always had to practice. It's a safe behavior, removes

you from normal life; but it's totally unrealistic for a healthy family environment.

Part of the reason I am like I am, is because I care deeply about what I'm doing and the responsibilities of my job. My coaching staff thinks I'm crazy for going in at 6:30 in the morning. And, if I sleep in the office, I feel they see I'm committed to my team, although it can also mean I don't have a balance in my life. It's one big cycle.

In the past few years though, I understood I needed to change. I knew it would take a lot more dedication than turning the phone off while I slept. My brother Cris asked me to go to a treatment center for a week that dealt with addictive behaviors of all types. He understood that I was used to taking care of everyone else, but not taking care of myself.

You don't know what you're getting into with one of these intensive sessions. I had my pager and a cell phone and I was using them all the way from the airport to the center. When I checked in, I was forced to put the cell phone and pager away. My first impression was the people there were taking it a bit too seriously. I didn't think I had any problems; but I thought I was surrounded by people who had problems.

The hardest part was being put in an environment where I couldn't help another person – in effect they told me that they were not going to let me be my own personality. All that responsibility starting from when I was a kid of dealing with everyone else's problems followed me throughout my life. Being the oldest of seven kids caught up with me. But, at the center, they said I didn't have to be responsible for other people. Of course, that was hard for me, and that week, I alternately felt guilty and relieved about my hectic life.

Ultimately, that week encouraged me to decide what was really important, and for whom and what I wanted to be responsible; I determined that I want to do my job but take extra time with my family. The reason to change my behavior was for my sons. Like many divorced or separated parents, it's much

harder not being in the same house. Children need both quality and quantity time. I think I miss them the most when things are going well with the team and when we're winning. They can't share my daily joys and I do wish I could see them more often than I do. But, when I'm with them, I'm really with them, physically and mentally – and yes, I do turn off the phones.

Part of taming workaholism is setting limits, saying no occasionally and not feeling like you can solve everyone else's problems. As far as taking on extra work, I'm still learning to say 'no.' If you're an enabler for others, try drawing back a bit. Not only does it allow someone else to be more responsible, but also it might release you of your need to control others. No matter what your addiction is, recognize that it may have too much control over your life and the lives of those who matter to you.

*"I see people who remain single and immerse themselves
in their work, and I don't know how they do it.
It's very important to be grounded somewhere."*

ALBERT BROOKS (ACTOR & DIRECTOR)

DO YOU HAVE ADDICTIVE BEHAVIORS?
HOW ARE THEY AFFECTING OTHERS?
ARE YOU BEING HONEST?
WHAT ARE THE SMALL STEPS YOU WILL
NOW TAKE TO CHANGE?

"When the general is morally weak and his discipline not strict, when his instructions and guidance are not enlightened, when there are no consistent rules to guide the officers and men and when the formations are slovenly, the army is in disorder."

THE ART OF WAR

The Art of Strategy

The importance and the idea of preparation has always appealed to me. I never shied away from doing homework and I understood early how crucial preparation is, no matter if it was a subject, a game or a business strategy. One Toronto reporter called me a prime example of a member "in good standing in the worrywart society." I learned that an investment in the preparation was as important as the game itself. For example, I've kept a notebook on players and plays for every year since 1978. I keep journals of on the job training, practices and phone numbers. In football, Cris is also known for his research and preparation and he gained that knowledge from watching me and seeing how preparedness improved my ability to play and coach well.

One of the books that helped me most understand the game and my role was *The Art of War*, originally written some 2,000 years ago and based on the ideas of Sun Tzu, a Chinese military

strategist. While military service is not of interest to me, and war itself is detestable, the book's philosophy is sound. It was given to me the first week when I was named interim coach in Toronto. I know it's widely read in the business world to understand basics such as competition, strategy and organization. That book gave me a foundation to organize all the material and thoughts I've been collecting over the years, which I had been doing by instinct.

The book's writings put into words the way I actually felt and I put forth quotes to my team. It even helped on the management side to centralize our thinking that "the battle" was going to start as soon as possible and we could not waste a day. We needed to get the players we wanted by the summer. We needed players who wanted to work and understand that part of the team success was based on their individual growth and conditioning in the summer. We put in conditioning programs that some people in Florida call "Toronto South," because we have a fitness program there. For players who have commitments elsewhere, the coaching staff will travel to any part of the country where they are located.

If you're making a $40 million investment in the stock market, you don't walk away for three months and not constantly review it and give it your attention. This attention is crucial because I'm taking a developing team, setting a foundation and trying to give them my vision. When the perception is the coach is not, or a team is not as talented as others, then you have to work harder. It's the only time they can't see you coming.

I quickly realized the instructions and principles in the book are what I've been informally collecting all along. I just needed to refine my thought process. From reading the book

"The enemy must not know where I intend to give attack, for if they do not know — they have to prepare in a great many places."

THE ART OF WAR

and referring to it often, I understood I needed a higher level of structured self-discipline, more so perhaps than some of my peers. I had begun to not only pull together these skills, but clarify my thinking in a structured way. This way of thinking and strategizing was already engendered in me.

What made the book's messages even more meaningful was that at that time, I was going through a personal crisis. I was still making the transition from player to coach, I was physically heavier than I'd ever been as I wasn't taking care of myself and I had dramatically changed my physical routine. I had made changes in my daily routine with no structure as to knowing what my day, week or what the month would bring.

Knowing I work best under structure and with a heightened sense of self-discipline, with my personal failures affecting me, I had lost all that kept me organized. *The Art of War* was really the kick in the pants that I needed to get back on track. As Charles Oakley says, "You can't talk about it, you have to be about it." And that philosophy has to be pervasive in all you do. It may feel weighty at times. But in reality it's a relief for me to understand this way of being is my basic personality, and how I function best.

Another way I employ a new strategy is in working effectively with management rather than seeing them as management *per se*. An almost hidden strength for our team is that we can't waste money. We're so very conscious of how much we could do with more funds. Maybe this is part of the Canadian conservatism and doing the best within the resources without being ostentatious, but most of the teams we play against spend more in salaries and marketing.

Our owners are doing the best they can on an uneven playing field – or court if you will – given the economic disadvantage of matching the Canadian dollar against the US dollar. There can be a detriment to being based in Canada when the game is based on a US dollar system. This means employing a management strategy that is more creative than just throwing money at a problem. This requires our staff to become better at everything in new creative ways, such as with the statistical evaluation of players to help us place less value on the old method of scouting. It also means creating innovative ways to promote the team.

Any coach is trying to climb the mountain of success and at some point he or she has to learn to adjust game-day strategy if it's not working within the game. As talented as teams are within

the NBA, a team cannot differentiate themselves from the rest unless they have three very good players. With them, you know their talent and experience is going to overcome 80 percent of any team's deficit. The length of time to bring some cohesion to a new team is not so much an issue, as the players who want to win have an internal force and commitment in that they don't just want to play the game, but want to win the game.

I do a lot of pre-emptive coaching and the more I do, the less fires I have to put out. If a player is having bad practices, I'm on him. I also film practice, so I can see who's giving the effort. I don't want to be yelling and screaming at the players, so I splice the film together and sit them down and ask them why I'm looking at what they're doing. I analyze what a guy's playing character is and how to best utilize his skills. The players are Gladiators and when they step on that court, their persona rises fully. My responsibility is leadership – to decode what's actually happening and use our resources, assets and talents to best competitive advantage.

I hope my coaching peers think well of me because hopefully they understand I'm going to work hard to make up their advantage of experience. I'm watching the coaches for clues, although there are times I get caught off guard. When we beat the Atlanta Hawks for the first time ever, I would not even think of copying that strategy going into the next game; that would be a formula for defeat as a coach, as there's time between the games to make adjustments.

This happened in one game with them in the 98/99 season. With a sense of doom, I knew five minutes into the game, the Hawks coach Lenny Wilkens had looked at every way to beat Toronto. He had prepared a strategy that was so much sounder than mine. That season my team was very hardworking, but we did not have enough veterans coming in from the bench to adjust quickly to a new game plan. His team was totally prepared. It's one thing to be prepared, but another to be prepared and exude the confidence they did from the first minute. They came in and

everything they did showed confidence. It's no wonder he's a Hall of Fame coach.

I actually felt fortunate I received that kind of lesson in a regular season game and not the playoffs. The difference in the playoff series is the second game – not the first as many might suspect. One team may have six or seven days of rest while the other has the playoff position determined on the last day. One team may have a ton of experience in the playoffs. But, if you win the second game there is a clear advantage. You get the home court advantage, so regardless of what happens, you come back to your home court for another game.

One would think the opening game of the season on your own home court would be an advantage and usually it is, but the opening of the 99/00 season was an example of where my strategy was faulty and not recoverable. The Boston Celtics potentially had three players that could score 30 points each in the game and my strategy was to keep those players from scoring. Meanwhile, the guy I forced to have the ball, made six out of six three-point shots, but didn't score much the following few games. I had to accept I was wrong and it points out that I don't think a person can be a good coach until he or she accepts they can be wrong. By accepting the blame to the team and through the media, I also wanted to take the heat off my players who were hurting from the opening night loss. The players have huge basketball IQs and are most extremely smart. If I tried to disrespect them by not dealing with the truth, it would only deteriorate our relationship of trust and truthfulness.

Although it's not strategy, just courtesy and good manners, one important thing is to thank people for their efforts and their involvement. By saying 'thank you' those two words combined together are extremely powerful.

For my job, which is always in an evaluation mode by the players, owners, fans, the league and even the average taxi driver, there's a higher price to pay compared to someone not in the public eye. The expectation of me is that there is no downtime.

My role is like a general in a war or a constant business strategist. And, I have to be because I'm competing with highly respected top coaches who can take something from any one of another 700 games of experience at a moment's notice to out-maneuver me. How I deal with the daily tests and how I prepare for the next challenges helps me every day.

"One who has few must prepare against the enemy – one who has many makes the enemy prepare against him."

THE ART OF WAR

DO YOU ALLOW YOURSELF THE ADVANTAGE OF PREPARATION?
DO YOU HAVE THE SELF-DISCIPLINE?
HOW CAN PREPARATION, DOING YOUR "HOMEWORK" OR
STRATEGY HELP YOU REACH YOUR GOALS?
CAN YOU LEARN FROM THE STRATEGIES OF OTHERS?

"He (Butch Carter) has done an excellent job. He has shown himself to be remarkably skilled at addressing problems head-on and shown a knack for walking the line between demanding the best out of players and not alienating them in the process."

LARRY BIRD (HEAD COACH, INDIANA PACERS)

Authority & Rules

Whether people like it or not, rules and authority are always going to be part of life, but it's important to realize that they are not meant to quash individual achievements or autonomy. Rules and authority are there to help guide people into accepted social norms, as a base to determine how to get along in society.

It's thought that in the sports world drug use, crime and boorish behavior exists, but it's not the norm. By far, most of the players are good people; it's just that they have a higher profile with the fans and media, and are subjected to higher social norms. As we are in the public eye, I feel that is fair. If we are public figures, we need to be conscious of the images we are portraying.

For a child who improves their environment and succeeds in professional sports, I find it a sad comment on life that they escape poverty and perhaps drug use, to be paid a lot of money and still clutter up their body with drugs. Using illegal drugs is

 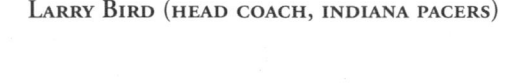

breaking the law. Rules in sports should mirror those in society. If a player uses violence to solve problems, or gets hooked into a bad crowd that doesn't respect norms, then you can't expect a kid to adhere to simple rules coaches use to maintain a team focus.

Rightly, fines and suspensions are now in place in the NBA for marijuana use, penalties exist for steroid use and there's disqualification for the use of harder drugs. Now that the NBA has instituted strict rules on drug use, it's better as everyone is following the same rulebook. Professional football has been testing players for drug use for years. If a player doesn't want to take a drug test, I think he or she should not be allowed to participate in professional sports. But, I do know drug use is not as widespread as people think, and certainly in my time I've observed a marked reduction.

Even as a player I was respectful of team rules. As a coach, I have a higher respect for rules and it's essential that I be a champion and support adherence. I know generally there's concern in society about kids not respecting rules, but in pro basketball, respecting rules is a fact of the business and the NBA itself is doing the right things in reinforcing standards and authority.

That's important as we are part of an industry that generates millions of dollars in creating an economic spinoff in the communities, by providing jobs, salaries and an infrastructure. Millions of dollars are invested in the sports industry and it provides entertainment. The NBA revenues are larger than many Fortune 500 companies. NBA Commissioner David Stern has done a good job in marketing the sport so that main street America can relate, whereas some players, such as Dennis Rodman, are intent on marketing themselves. The NBAs top stars have been mass marketed so well, those with moderate talent seek other ways to attract attention. They may not be able to do it with talent, so they do it with flash.

When I came to the league you could even wear whatever colored shoes you wanted or different socks, but now the increased professionalism is better in all ways for the sport.

Similarly, tattoos are now in; it's a way of a player differentiating himself from the group and like banning bandannas in football, there's a message there that if you want to participate, you have to play by the rules. Earrings are also gone and players are not allowed to wear jewelry in the game anyway. This just mirrors life. If you are a lawyer, you likely wouldn't wear a halter top to court and if you're a teacher you'd likely not be late to class every day.

But authority and rules have to be applied fairly. I used to hate it when I was playing in the pros and sitting on the bench, not playing for a few games. By the time you really knew the coach was upset with you over something and asked him, it would be too late to work on whatever it was you could have corrected. I never liked the idea of a coach disappearing into the office and thinking he was right all the time, because that approach never gave those players an opportunity to work on themselves. While my players have basic rules to follow; there's a direct understanding that I'm going to address any problems up front, but I still have the authority.

As a coach, I don't hang out socially with the players or I lose everything I've gained in the gym. Nothing is worth losing their respect. There have been times I've been headed into a restaurant and there'll be a group of players there. The other coaches and I will turn around and go somewhere else to give them their space. They need a break from me as an authority figure every once in awhile.

One problem with kids is that they are so encouraged to cultivate individuality, to the point of not always learning to follow rules. In high school, we used to allow players to have one part in their hair and their hair couldn't be longer than the coach's hair. They'd get a few complaints, and we'd point out that was entirely the purpose; complaining doesn't make you any better, so get with the program. By using small rules such as dress codes, you hope to get individuals to buy in to what's best for the group.

There are many types of "coaches" in a person's life. Kids also learn to listen to a coach from the kind of training they're getting

at home, and from their extended families. They should be taught simple social scripts such as waiting their turn, saying 'please' and 'thank you' and being good mannered to other people. A good relationship with a coach parallels the model of respect the kids see at home. Kids learn respect through how they are treated by adults and their peers, and shown the way by respecting rules and authority.

"I've always had respect for Butch because he treats you with respect. He expects the best out of you. But, if you're not playing well, he'll address it as a man should. You can do nothing but respect that."

JOHN THOMAS (PLAYER, TORONTO RAPTORS)

WHAT RULES ARE IN YOUR LIFE?
HOW DO THESE HELP YOU?
DO YOU PAY ATTENTION TO SOCIAL NORMS?
ARE YOU RESPECTFUL OF AUTHORITY FIGURES?

"Anyone who said he wasn't afraid during the civil rights movement was either a liar or without imagination. I was scared all the time."

JAMES FARMER (CIVIL RIGHTS ACTIVIST)

Being Scared

I'm not sure why, but people seem to not want to admit that they are scared sometimes. Maybe it's an athlete thing or a male thing, but it's important to know there is nothing wrong with being scared. I think people are actually more scared of failing, so inaction becomes a bailout. And some people even are afraid of being successful – maybe because they feel they don't deserve it. They downplay their success by saying they were in the right place at the right time or were lucky.

Believing there is nothing wrong is one way to talk yourself into ignoring your fear. That emotion – no matter what it is you're afraid of – tends to dominate and paralyze you. It can control your life so much that you think your whole life is falling apart. It is a slippery slope that you must stop yourself from sliding down. And you have to put in perspective the magnitude of what you are facing; there's not as much riding on a ball game as there is in the challenges of real life.

I once drove by a gas station that had a sign outside where someone changes the letters and posts a thought of the week. One week, the sign read "Falling isn't failing, but staying down is." I remember thinking that simple phrase that someone chose to put on the sign at that gas station probably gave more hope to people that week than any pep talk.

You can't be afraid to win the game whether in sports or life. I always knew that as an athlete I'd have more chances at the end of the game – some guys just would not want to take the shot to win as there would be so much pressure on them. Charles Oakley isn't one of those guys – he thrives on the pressure. Being the oldest child in my family, I had to make decisions for everyone and take action to solve problems. That's why at the end of a game I felt comfortable going for that last shot and can now say I was seldom thrown off or scared at the end of a game. But, it wasn't always that way.

There was a big high school game when I was 15 years old and I was scared to death. The other guys were bigger and meaner looking and the crowd was hostile. I missed a free throw and it helped the other team to win the game. It hurt me to no end and I promised myself I would never be that scared again. All summer long I practiced my free throws and I always mouthed the team's name. That's likely why I hate anyone on my team being afraid at the end of the game, because the person who is scared to perform is not going to win anything.

Preparation is something you can do no matter what you are afraid of, whether it is an upcoming test or a talk with your boss. One technique I used was visualization. The act of closing your eyes and mentally walking yourself through specific actions and memorizing, helps you create a positive outcome. Two days before the game I'd get a good night's sleep because I knew the night before a game I might not sleep well. It may sound simple, but try that whether you have a speech to give, a job interview, or a new class at school. If you can train yourself to be relaxed the day prior to the day before a meaningful event, you're storing up

the physical resources you may need to draw on later.

Although others may have been more gifted physically, I would put in more preparation and practice. Although I might have been scared, I'd mentally prepare myself for always getting in the game. If I heard a team's play called, I'd memorize it, go through the plays, look at everything and focus on what I needed to do.

That mental preparation is equally important to physical preparation for a basketball game, so why wouldn't that be true for anything in life? People told me to stop taking the game so seriously, but I feel if you are mentally engaged as well as physically, you are prepared and you can overcome feeling scared. That's also very true with much in daily life. Everyone feels afraid or is scared about something; whether it is rational or irrational. Taking small physical and mental steps to give you an edge over your fears is a good way to overcome what makes you scared.

"If you're never scared or embarrassed or hurt,
it means you never take any chances."

JULIA SOREL (AUTHOR)

WHAT MAKES YOU FEEL SCARED?
ARE THESE SITUATIONS YOU CAN CONTROL?
DO YOU NEED THE HELP OF OTHERS?
HOW WILL YOU PREPARE YOURSELF FOR THE FUTURE?

"Every person is born into the world to do something unique and something distinctive and if he or she does not do it, it will never be done."

BENJAMIN E. MAYS (EDUCATOR)

Believing in Dreams

I am a product of failure. My father was defeated and a quitter, who ignored his family and responsibilities. My mother just never quit. I don't know where my mother got her spirit from; it would have been so easy to bail. I don't think it even entered my mind to be like my father, so I just never accepted defeat.

It was my dream when I was young to make my life matter, to rise up in society. It was my dream to have a comfortable life, to take care of my family and provide a better life for my children. I think these are essentially simple and universal goals. There is nothing glamorous about them. Being the eldest, I had a heightened sense of responsibility, but I think that would have been true no matter in what order I had been born among my siblings.

I remember going to school and not having a lunch or money to buy food. I was trying to be so proud that I wouldn't even take a free lunch. I'd go to football practice on an empty stomach and

I was mad at my circumstances. I was mad at the kids who didn't appreciate and understand what they had – that they had something as simple as three good meals a day.

I have been knocked down, I have been tripped up and I have stumbled. Every time I got knocked down, I found some way to get up. But, the difference with me and some of the kids I went to school with, is I had a clear dream of a better life and I found some way to believe in my dreams. I found some way to put my dreams into reality by participating in them and taking small steps to achieve them. And, you need to learn this lesson in self-reliance because life can be very cruel.

The decisions you make at 15, 16, or 17 years old can have a very negative impact on the rest of your life, or these decisions can launch you into your adulthood with promise and hope. At 17, I decided I just couldn't hang out any more wasting my life. I was determined to make my life count.

You have your own unique dreams; no one can take them away from you. And when you have dreams – no matter how seemingly impossible – that's what keeps you motivated. You must have an inner sense that your life matters and you are put on earth to fulfill very special dreams, which are uniquely yours. Whether you are young or old, you must participate in your dreams – and not only the dream, but take little baby steps to make your dream come true. At any age, it's not too late to start. When I was a 15 year old high school sophomore, I made up a little poster board and cut out pictures of my favorite sports stars to paste on it. I put it up in my room and it provided me a visual reminder of how I could achieve my dream.

Some people write in journals, some put up riveting posters but it's the process of writing and documenting your dreams which bring them clearly into focus and provide you with a constant prompting.

A living example of how you can participate in achieving your dream is a player we signed in the 99/00 season. Tyrone (Muggsy) Bogues grew up in the projects in Baltimore's inner

city. At seven years old, he knew he wanted to play professional sports and like many kids, felt it was the way out of poverty. Although wrestling was his first love, he got involved in many sports and found his skill growing yearly, while his body stopped at 5 foot 3 inches. But, Muggsy felt basketball was his dream. Coming from a family small in stature, when he told his parents he planned on being in the NBA, they nodded politely, but also supported him. Even though the average NBA player is 6 foot 7 inches, not once did they try to talk him out of his dream during those years through junior and high school to college. In fact, he earned his nickname because of his habit of taking his taller pals off guard and "mugging" the ball from them.

Against criticism, regular putdowns and a tough environment that forced him to have to prove himself daily, Muggsy kept his dream alive. He didn't care what his detractors thought; he just became more motivated to fulfill his dream. As a point guard, one of Muggsy's jobs is to set up plays for his teammates, which he does exceedingly well, being the NBAs all-time best in the assists-to-turnover ratio. With the 99/00 year his 13th NBA season, Muggsy has inspired fans who remain intrigued and are still amazed at his determination. At 140 pounds and speedy, he breaks through the mental models of what people think NBA players should look like.

With a strong visualization of where he wanted to be in life, Muggsy's dream encourages others. He funds the Muggsy Bogues Learning Center in Baltimore to help people overcome the individual adversities they face, whether it's adequately supporting a family or getting educated to change jobs. I asked him if he ever gets jaded about looking into the eyes of a young fan who thinks he's achieved the "height of success." Muggsy said no, if it's possible for him to inspire people to believe in their dreams he's happy. While he may never win a Nobel Prize or other worldly acclaim, a person can't get much more admirable than gently reaching into a young child's heart and mind, and encouraging him or her to believe in a dream.

If I can overcome being the eldest of seven children with all its responsibilities, and my mother very often being the only parent there – if I can overcome that, then any one of you can overcome the obstacles put in your way. If you fall, don't consider it a failure – consider it a stumble and just pick yourself up. Have the courage to live your dream – no one else is going to live it your way.

> *"The dream is real, my friends. The failure to make it work is the unreality."*
>
> TONI CADE BAMBARA (AUTHOR)

WHAT WERE YOUR DREAMS WHEN YOU WERE YOUNGER?
DID YOU ACHIEVE MOST OR ALL OF THEM?
HOW HAVE YOUR DREAMS CHANGED OVER THE YEARS?
WHAT ARE SOME OF YOUR NEW DREAMS? NOTE YOUR TOP
THREE, HOW YOU CAN ACHIEVE THEM AND WHEN.

"Unfortunately, in a long life one gets barnacled over with the mere shells of friendship and it is difficult without hurting oneself to scrape them off."

BERNARD BERENSON (ART CRITIC)

Beware of Cowards

A painful lesson to learn at any age is how to make friends and also knowing just how and why friendships and acquaintances unravel. It's crucial to make a distinction between sincere friends and acquaintances seeking to exploit the relationship for what you can bring to their lives. A true friendship is built on shared experiences to mutual benefit. A friend loves you for who you are, warts and all, through good experiences and bad, whereas a casual companion or acquaintance seems to like certain parts of you. Developing and maintaining friendships presents certain challenges when you've got a grueling travel schedule.

To complicate relationships, when push comes to shove, you have to put people where they actually are in your life. People whom you thought were friends, you understand later had befriended you as they wanted something from you, not necessarily because they wanted to contribute positively to your life.

Many cannot and do not understand that this is a method of control and maintaining an illusion of superiority. I think these people are cowards, who will do damage to others by their destructive words and underhanded actions. But people forgive their bullying behavior because they have power. An example of this type of person is Bobby Knight, head coach of the basketball team at Indiana University.

When I was an 18 year old freshman at Indiana, Knight gave me a copy of the wonderful Rudyard Kipling poem *If*, which illustrates the positive and negatives of the journey through life. It speaks of hypocrisy and duplicity in a friendship. It's ironic Knight handed it to me, as we are now estranged.

However, the poem remains a poignant source of strength for me. While Knight motivates in a detrimental manner and people do learn from negative lessons, I realized later that he was like many dictators – selfish and ruthless and you just can't get too close to challenging or questioning them. They always have some overt or insidious way of maintaining control and use threats to hold you back. This is different from being a mentor, as a mentor wants the best for you, but doesn't use intimidation and threats as methods to help you develop.

If – by Rudyard Kipling

If you can keep your head when all about you
Are losing theirs and blaming it on you;
If you can trust yourself when all men doubt you,
But make allowance for their doubting too:
If you can wait and not be tired by waiting,
Or, being lied about, don't deal in lies,
Or being hated don't give way to hating,
And yet don't look too good, nor talk too wise;

Although with media reports and the actions I witnessed, I don't know if Knight is a racist, but I know he does not like educated strong-willed blacks. He is the kind of man who implies a man should not stand up and be a man; should not have an intelligent opinion. I feel it would be fair to say that he does not like the fact that Cris and I are professionally successful.

This all started when "God" stopped practice early one day. I first heard my mother call Knight "God" during my recruitment. During recruitment, Knight promised he'd be fair to

my teammates and me and we would not be subject to segregated behavior. When we were recruited, we thought we'd left these segregated situations behind.

One bad day, Knight first threw me out of practice, then threw everyone out, but Knight called me back onto the court while the guys were heading to the locker room. He ripped me up and down. He was still in a rage in the locker room 15 minutes later, going up and down the line. Knight yelled at one of the players that he would end up like "all the rest of the niggers in Chicago, including your

If you can dream—and not make dreams your master;
If you can think—and not make thoughts your aim,
If you can meet with Triumph and Disaster
And treat those two impostors just the same:.
If you can bear to hear the truth you've spoken
Twisted by knaves to make a trap for fools,
Or watch the things you gave your life to, broken,
And stoop and build'em up with worn—out tools;

brothers!" An assistant coach, grabbed him and pulled him from the room, while Knight screamed that "I don't have to f****** apologize!" I'll never forget looking at that assistant coach, who I greatly admired as a person, yet with Knight's outburst, he couldn't speak up; he couldn't say anything.

When you tell a kid he's going to be like every "nigger" in Chicago, how far is that over the line of inappropriate and cowardly behavior? Knight felt he was at such a superior level that he could make a statement like that to a player in front of his teammates and he had no obligation to apologize to him or the rest of the black players. In effect, not only was Knight talking to that player, but he was also talking to his two captains. Both of us came from families with many children.

His words and anger affected me, because he was overtly talking about all of us; the eight black players in that locker room and essentially all the black players he had ever coached. All these players had put money in his pockets and helped win Big Ten and National Championships, yet he was hypocritical and deliberately chose to say what he truly felt about us.

We all got dressed quickly and scattered, knowing that his tirade could have been directed at any one of us. I felt sorry for

that individual player, but he said not to worry about it as he had decided to leave the next year. This talented player could have chosen any college, with a scholarship, but he had chosen to go to Indiana. Knight had shown his deepest, darkest thoughts and resentment to him and everyone in the locker room had witnessed the display.

Knight never did apologize – that day, nor in the week or months afterward. It was as if it had never even dawned on him that his behavior and that incident might not only be unacceptable, but hurtful in the long run.

Even after the years have passed and I was doing everything possible to move away from that incident, it haunted me. A former Indiana teammate who was also in the locker room that day, sat down with me at a restaurant a couple of years back. Randy Wittman is now head coach of Cleveland Cavaliers and he was upset with me, saying he heard I'd been saying Knight is racist. I had never talked about the incidents at Indiana I'm describing – I've never mentioned them to family members, friends, nor discussed it with those teammates.

If you can make one heap of all your winnings
And risk it on one turn of pitch–and–toss,
And lose, and start again at your beginnings,
And never breathe a word about your loss:
If you can force your heart and nerve and sinew
To serve your turn long after they are gone,
And so hold on when there is nothing in you
Except the Will which says to them: "Hold on!"

I asked Randy, 'You sat there in the locker room and heard the same thing I did. What part of it did you not understand?' Even if he didn't think the comment was racist, was Knight just having a bad day? How did I end up getting the blame for what Knight said? I left there thinking that here's this guy coaching in the NBA and how is he ever going to be fair to his black players if he takes that stand on that statement? He did it because of intimidation and widespread acceptance of Knight's behavior. This reminded me again of the poem's validity and especially the first two lines.

Another incident that happened after a practice in my first season was the final straw in having any trust in Knight. That

year he had also denounced a former player in the locker room in front of our team, who was in his rookie year with the Milwaukee Bucks. The team was visiting Indiana for a game with the Indiana Pacers and the player had taken the time to drive down to talk to Knight. He was evidently having personal problems and thought he was discussing it in private. Knight immediately came down from this meeting and talked to the team and told us the intimate details. With no thought of discretion or sensitivity, Knight shamelessly used their discussion as an example of why we needed to listen to him in making decisions to avoid making mistakes.

If you can talk with crowds and keep your virtue,
Or walk with Kings—nor lose the common touch,
If neither foes nor loving friends can hurt you,
If all men count with you, but none too much:
If you can fill the unforgiving minute
With sixty seconds' worth of distance run,
Yours is the Earth and everything that's in it,
And—which is more—you'll be a Man, my son!

That's what turned me totally away from Knight – doing what he did to that man was cowardly. And it was totally unnecessary. It was self-serving – it was none of our business what was going on in this player's life and I was even more disgusted since this player had helped to recruit me to Indiana. I left the locker room in a furious state. This man had trusted Knight with the most intimate details of his personal life and Knight used it as a tool to make himself look good.

Half the guys in the locker room didn't even know the player personally and after the incident of Knight's locker room explosion at the black player combined with this, I knew I was never to trust this man with anything going on in my life. Not only was Knight clearly not a friend, he was a self-serving coward who masqueraded as a confidante.

If Knight was angry, he usually was angry at me first as I was the team captain. With two starters out with injuries, it showed in our early record. Knight knew I was the first in conditioning, but told me I was to be the sixth man, and was not even allowed to compete for a starting spot that season. We were in a position to win the Big Ten Championship, on the strength of Isiah

Thomas. Luckily, his sheer talent was so impressive that Knight overlooked situations, and it was a constant pleasure to me that he would have to bend to the will of Isiah. And, Isiah did not let Knight stop him from developing his natural talent.

Still, he'd take me out of the game if anyone else made a mistake. After one particular game where he benched me and let us lose the game, I called a friend who worked at the university. He said that if I was going to listen to everything he said, I wasn't going to be able to play. He was right, and I'll bet he gave that speech many times. I just decided not to listen to Knight and I overcame whatever he put in my way.

Most players were forced to play a level of basketball they might not have reached otherwise, and a lot of good players have come out of Indiana. There are no gray areas there – you're either a successful player or you're not.

How did these players – these men – swallow their pride to accomplish a more important goal of teamwork, winning and taking instruction? We buried any feelings of personal boldness and became a versatile, strong and powerful team. Some people do well in a prescriptive, militaristic environment where they adapt well to being told what to do. Some don't and bury their personal feelings, which is destructive. In this case, winning wasn't everything.

Knight always used to say, "I've forgotten more about basketball than you'll know." That's especially true since he's a better politician than he is a coach. For example, he said his practices were closed, but then we'd see his favorite trustee of the moment or the president of the university at practice, so we knew it would be an easy practice and we'd get the hard practice later.

He always told us that when you win games, people continue to accept whatever you do and he has proved that over and over again. Swearing was a common way for him to express his anger but that was tolerated as well as his explosive physical actions such as throwing or kicking objects. I understood him so well because he was so predictable; one of the most predictable people

who have been part of my life. He understands most people are weak and shy away from confrontation.

When incidents like these happen in life to you, or if you are an observer, you think by being quiet or with time it will go away. But it doesn't go away. Continuously throughout my process to become a head coach, in college and in the pros, people fed off the fact that I did not have a strong relationship with Knight.

One athletic director told me in an interview for his head coach's job that he thought he needed Knight's recommendation. I was up for a college job and it was one of the few times I've lost my temper. I specifically told him that if he needed Knight's recommendation, I didn't want the job. The guy talked to Knight and I didn't get the job because Knight discouraged him from hiring me. I played for Knight, was his captain, and I graduated on time, yet he had the power to defeat me professionally. But the way the system is set up in the United States, you can pick up the phone and assassinate someone's character, as it's the politics of the game. Interviewers don't check because it's the perception that counts.

For some reason, Knight can't acknowledge he's one of those old-style, intimidating personalities who's got seasoned athletes and coaching peers quaking in their sneakers rather than talk about him publicly. It's understandable as many bide their time and are worried about the repercussions of confrontation. The fact is, when you deny stories, you actually then are accepting and perpetuating cowardly behavior. It's a detriment to the public, the league, players, and the families of athletes being recruited. Dark private thoughts are just that, and the ones who are hurting are the people who don't acknowledge his harmful private behavior.

I don't for a moment expect others to acknowledge these particular incidents as we've all got a lot on the line, but I wouldn't be true to myself if I kept it hidden. Some people say "forgive and forget," but if we all did that, we'd forget crimes and the large acts of irresponsibility and abuse. Besides, it reinforces

the best way I've learned how to deal with controversy and static; deal with it head on and move on.

I mentioned earlier that I don't believe you rise up by stepping on people; your job in life is to help people rise up as you rise. Unfortunately, there are people who stomp on you as you rise. Don't accept it. You may have to wait a few years before you understand what was happening and how to make it right for you, but don't hold on to destructive relationships or thoughts.

And of course, beware of cowards.

"You are not judged by the height you have risen,
but from the depth you have climbed."

FREDERICK DOUGLASS (LEADER & AUTHOR)

WHO ARE THE PEOPLE IN YOUR LIFE YOU CONSIDER
TRUE FRIENDS?
WHO ARE ACQUAINTANCES?
DO YOUR FEEL SOME OF YOUR FRIENDS AND ACQUAINTANCES
ARE SO BECAUSE OF WHAT YOU GIVE THEM (FOR EXAMPLE:
EMOTIONAL OR FINANCIAL SUPPORT) THAT MAY BE ONE-SIDED?
DO YOU TREAT YOUR TRUE FRIENDS WELL?

"When a man angers you, he conquers you."

TONI MORRISON (AUTHOR)

Channeling Your Anger

Being scared, discouraged and how you handle dealing with these emotions is closely tied into how you handle expressing emotions – especially your anger. It's your anger that can cause repercussions depending on how it's channeled. Some people use their anger destructively such as in hurting others, breaking something, or publicly causing destruction. I think anger is better channeled into positive action.

As of the end of the 99/00 NBA season, I still own the record – 16 years now – for the most points scored in a NBA game in overtime. In 1984, I scored 14 points for the Indiana Pacers, breaking a record set by Earl "the Pearl" Monroe on February 6, 1970 and tied by Joe Caldwell less than two weeks later. One reason that I made those points was that I learned to channel my anger the right way.

Even with Larry Bird playing for Boston, the Pacers were up 14 points over the Celtics, but our coach took the starters out of

the game and put in subs. Because we weren't put back in soon enough, the Celtics tied the game and it went to overtime. I was furious the coach didn't put us back in to save the game during regulation time and the whole crowd was angry. I had played seven years in the state of Indiana and never heard such booing. The fans were right. I was furious that the coach could do that – we had earned the lead, and we wanted to win the game.

Rather than getting mad at the coach or the opponents, I channeled my anger into my work and nothing was going to keep me down. I emotionally tuned everything out, stole the tip, had a quick three-point play and basically directed the team. If anyone was going to shoot the ball, it was going to be me.

After winning that game, I had to go sit in the shower for quite awhile, because I had so much emotion still coursing through me. I think my reaction made the younger players a little scared though – rather than seeing me ebullient and happy, they saw me dispirited. I was thinking about was how close we had come to failing as a team and how close I came to failing to do what I knew to be the best thing to do.

"Butch Carter is a man who downplays big moments in franchise history. He never appears all that happy after a win. He never appears to be fuming after a loss."

THE NATIONAL POST,
APRIL 27, 1999

When I was a little kid I had a really bad temper. I remember being eight years old and getting into an argument at school that ended as a shoving match in the playground. I was being taken into the principal's office and he was going to give me a paddling. I thought I was smart and took off home and poured out the story to my mother, expecting sympathy. But, she marched me right back to school and held me down so they could paddle me. She wanted me to learn how out of control my temper was and she didn't want me to be like my father, using anger to settle arguments. From an early age I had to learn to control my temper and also to find another way to settle conflict. That was a gradual process, as I'd get very angry inside about different things and have to find ways to channel it. Now I find it easier to get over things and move on or settle

issues. That's not to say I don't feel intense emotion. It means I've taken control of it and choose to direct it in a way that works for me.

I'm big on not saying anything when I'm mad – there is some relief of emotion if you throw your weight around and bust up something or tell people off, but that's not me and I don't think that's right. In the Celtics game, the truth about having to address my anger was that I knew I wasn't right unless I won the game. Learning how to channel my anger then makes me a better coach now, especially to the young players who may not know how to use anger in a positive way.

I think sometimes you have got to reign in your emotion. Even though I'm known as a pretty intense guy, I don't show a lot of emotion during games whether we're winning or losing. As an example, a sign was pointed out to me by one of the staff at the Air Canada Centre, our new home as of the 98/99 season. There, held aloft by some astute young fan, was a hand-painted sign reading "SMILE Butch." Well, I did have to laugh and I think the cameras caught that one.

Those who know me well can't often tell if I'm ready to bust up laughing or to shut them down – I've just got one of those faces that hides emotion. I'm not saying that's good – that's the way I am and largely part of my upbringing. I don't feel comfortable expressing my emotion, but that's not the same thing as not feeling it.

If you're one of those people though who display one emotion while you're feeling another, think about the mixed messages you are giving others. Give some thought to how you can channel your negative emotions into something positive. If you've had a bad day at work don't transfer the anger you feel toward your boss onto your kids. Don't get annoyed at some test by telling yourself it doesn't matter, only to fail it.

Train yourself to address the issue head-on and deal with it. It will become routine and rather than being hot-headed, you'll start to develop ways to think your way out of situations.

"Grab the broom of anger and drive off the beast of fear."

ZORA NEALE HURSTON (AUTHOR)

WHAT SITUATIONS MAKE YOU ANGRY?
WHAT DO YOU USUALLY DO TO RESOLVE THEM?
DO YOU PICK FIGHTS? IGNORE ISSUES?
HOW CAN YOU CHANNEL ANGER INTO POSITIVE RESULTS?
HOW DO YOU WANT TO REACT DIFFERENTLY TO TRIGGERS?

"How far you go in life depends on you being tender with the young, compassionate with the aged, sympathetic with the striving and tolerant of the weak and strong. Because someday in life you will have several of these."

GEORGE WASHINGTON CARVER (EDUCATOR & RESEARCHER)

Community Service

When I first started playing in the NBA I would spend my summers giving motivational speeches and I always had a higher goal of trying to inspire more kids than my brothers and sisters. It helps me keep my balance and remember where I came from. I also like my sons to see the contrast in how they live with how others live – not to embarrass anyone, but to ensure my sons have compassion for others and subtly show them they are being raised in the best situation possible. If children do not learn compassion when they are young and begin to give back into their communities, just how do you teach compassion when our children become adults?

We attend many charitable events as a team and as individuals, and I encourage involvement as I think that's partly my role as an ambassador for the team. There are many unique programs that reach out into communities. The Toronto Raptors have been very progressive with the players being out in the community and

some of the innovative programs such as the Reading Time Out Program, where we recommend favorite books, and the Slam Dunk Youth Violence Program.

Right from when we start to talk about acquiring a player, we're also looking for guys of character who will give back into the community. As a team we tend to be out there a lot and all the guys do charity work, whether it's golf tournaments, youth events or visiting children in hospitals. Even during the 98/99 lockout some of the players paid their own way to attend community events.

I do enjoy these events and feel blessed to be able to give something back, but I also feel very uncomfortable drawing attention to myself in getting personal recognition for supporting something worthwhile. Similarly, when I make a donation or buy a high school team some supplies, I don't want personal recognition. It's just something I think people should do as part of their covenants with each other and as contributing members of their communities.

I think charitable activities dovetail with a push for professional sports athletes, across the board, to become better role models. Cynics might say it's a marketing tool designed to keep up the profile, but honestly, we don't need profile if it's just to get in the faces of fans. We want to do these events because a smile on a kid's face cannot be faked and we all need that one-on-one to connect where we can do some good.

We also happen to think we are good role models and good human beings. With the public and media exposure, people think of those in sports as role models and they can't help but see us as trying to be part of the community and helping out. As athletes, we are grateful for the opportunity to play. We understand that our time is fleeting and we have a love of the game we try to transmit to others.

While some of the players may say they are not and don't want to be role models, you don't always know who's watching you. A lot of guys can stand up and say "hey I came from there

and I'm now doing this and living here and want to go back and return something." Kids need positive models, and study after study shows the positive influence that sports has on a young person's life. There are so many good attributes; learning how to be a team player, being with others who take care of themselves physically, being with adult coaches who guide you, or breaking away from environments potentially poisoned by drug use or crime. Even how we use words has meaning. One of my favorite examples of the power of words is from city planner and author Jane Jacobs who said if you call apartments "projects" they become the projects, but if you call them "communities" they become communities.

I attend some 25 charitable events a year and always seem to be on the go. And, it's not just the Toronto area we visit. One of my most memorable visits was to Cole Harbour High School in Halifax/Dartmouth on Canada's East Coast. Because racial conflicts are so rare in Canada, I remember hearing of the school's incident of racial tension in the media the year before. This tension had demoralized the school and it had almost closed, but the students, teachers and administrators seized it back. One label the school did not want was to be considered the poster school of racism.

When someone from the team was asked to visit during their Diversity Week in October 1998, it was during the lockout, but I wanted to go. I thought I could share some of my thoughts and wisdom on the value of education, the need for racial harmony, and to impart what little I know about life to the some 1,000 students. I also wanted to make other visits, such as to the local children's hospital.

Nova Scotia holds the oldest indigenous black community in Canada and Cole Harbour, an area of some 60,000 people, lies a bit to the east of this beautiful province's main city. The school was holding a special week to honor diversity and had planned many morale-boosting and school spirit activities to launch the

new school year. I spoke on the Friday to wrap up the week. I was also to present awards to deserving students whose efforts toward racial harmony were to be recognized.

I didn't think I was going to go and reach them all. I was once a knuckle-headed young teenager who didn't know everything and thought I did. I thought whoever would listen might pick up a thing or two out of the whole talk to sustain them and that's who I tried to reach. If I could energize the day or year of even ten kids and they could accept my message, then that was benefit enough to me.

When I walked through the front doors, I first saw a display case filled with sports trophies, much like any high school. Then I saw a sign in the main office that said it all to me, so I knew my point would be heard. The sign displayed said, "There are no shortcuts to life's greatest achievements." I saw many other tangible and intangible signs that this school was determined to put this racial event behind them and move on with a solution based on getting the students involved.

I spoke at two packed assemblies about belief in oneself, the hardships I've endured, the great moments, hard work and how to overcome obstacles. I also spoke about peer pressure and how hard it is when you're a teenager, to make decisions that may affect a lifetime. One of the students asked me who my role model was, and I was proud and emotional to tell them it was my mother.

> *"I will never forget the energy in that room; the feeling that this event was special and was meant to be shared by all of us. When the student is ready the teacher will appear. What Butch didn't realize was that he also was the student."*
>
> KAREN PETCOFF,
> MAPLE LEAF SPORTS &
> ENTERTAINMENT LTD.

I'm still not sure why this particular school had an impact on me, but I genuinely think they were grateful I came to see them. They tried to understand my experiences and I do believe the visit had a lasting impact on many of them. I personally donated $10,000, which was an impromptu gesture and pretty much shocked everyone in the room including me. But, I did it because

I was filled with emotion at what the school was trying to accomplish and of the hope of the students. I really wanted to put my money where my mouth was in supporting what these teens were trying to do to change the image of their school and build it back. Between representatives of the school and I, we decided the money would go to fund four student scholarships based on the most thoughtful essays on racial harmony.

One of the teachers told me that the students had never given an unsolicited standing ovation to a speaker before and that I had really touched something in those kids. I was so pleased to be able to shake the hands of so many young adults that day and feel the positive energy in those rooms. That to me is the best of community service; an experience shared, wisdom passed on, energy given and received and hopefully, long lasting effects.

Rather than thinking the world owes us something, let's see how much we can put back into the world with funding, a smile, a kind gesture or an act of genuine caring that desires no recompense.

"Too often we underestimate the power of a touch, a smile, a kind word, a listening ear, an honest compliment, or the smallest act of caring, all of which have the potential to turn a life around."

LEO BUSCAGLIA (AUTHOR & EDUCATOR)

HOW DO YOU CONTRIBUTE TO YOUR COMMUNITY?
WHAT TYPE OF WISDOM OR SKILLS CAN YOU SHARE?
WHAT SMALL ACTS OF KINDNESS CAN YOU DO EVERY DAY?
DO YOU DO THESE ACTS GENUINELY OR DO YOU EXPECT TO
GET SOMETHING IN RETURN?

"I have come to believe that until one learns to love and respect oneself, one will not be able to control one's life and destiny. When you have self-esteem, you will not allow anybody to relegate you to poverty or misery or unhappiness."

MAXINE WATERS (POLITICIAN)

The Difference Between Ego & Self-Esteem

Whether you excel in a business discipline, sports, or life, there's a fine line between having positive self-esteem and having an ego. I think having good self-esteem is vital, especially when you're trying to learn a new task, as you take calculable risks in your efforts to grow and learn. Ego is vital to a professional athlete – it's often what keeps he or she motivated. On the other hand, ego can be a self-destructive sensation that often goes along with fleeting fame and an inflated sense of self-importance.

I think having good self-esteem is a sign of maturity. It means seeing the larger picture and where you fit in, rather than pursuing just your own selfish goals. It means holding off immediate self-gratification for the rewards that may come later. It's the perseverance of getting a job done, overcoming adversity and suffering some of the slings and arrows of setbacks.

Self-esteem is the ability to control and use your emotions appropriately, to consult with others and cull their wisdom and ability. It's the innate or acquired ability to acknowledge and change your shortcomings and when you are right, not rub your opponent's nose in it. It means being reliable, dependable and responsible rather than neglecting your obligations because of a momentary flash of anger or passion. It means being able to be counted on and standing by your decisions. It means moving on, rather than holding onto insults against you, or mistakes you have made which still hold you back.

Self-esteem means being able to deal with personal slights as when other kids taunt you and make fun of you – and your peers at any age can be so hurtful. Like many kids who are physically different in even the smallest of ways, I was taunted for the size of my feet when I was young. I wore size 13 shoes when I was 13 years old and had to endure people heckling me with remarks such as, "Butch, let me borrow your shoes so I can go skiing!"

Ego is none of those things – ego is the driver and the passion that makes you unique, but ego is like wearing a suit so bright so they can see you coming. It gives people more time to build up barriers. But, of course, I want my players to have an ego. I'm not trying to break them – just mature them. The tough part of my job is deciding what players to play and believe me, it's a problem I'm happy to have. We have good players and while I want to give them all exposure and playing time, they need to also work to achieve the team goals.

When I played basketball, I didn't want to get caught up in believing the personal hype as I'd seen so many athletes reading about how good they were one month and how they failed the next. I watched my high school teammates getting caught up in reading things that had been written about them in the local newspaper. They knew if they didn't get their grades in school then the opportunity to be in the paper would disappear. What ended up happening was they lost perspective and became dependent on what others thought of their performance. They

internalized those reviews for their own satisfaction or concern and ended up not making good decisions.

So, since I didn't like what I saw as a teenager, I simply didn't read the sports sections. As I was growing up, I'd seen so many athletes getting their heads twisted by reading that they were the greatest thing one day and on the skids the next. That haunted the way they felt about themselves.

Athletes are no different from people in any profession when it comes to having an ego, but sports figures have more public exposure so the public sees the expression of ego more. It is just reflective of society that there are going to be outlandish players who are very public figures, but most players have rather quiet natures and healthy self-esteem. Some of them are fortunate because when their ego got out of hand at an early age, someone helped them deflate it.

As a professional athlete, getting traded normally indicates you did not have enough value to be kept. It creates a heightened sense of rejection for an athlete; much like going through a divorce. You spend all that time and effort validating your identity as part of something larger than yourself, then have to remember you are an individual. You seek to find worth as part of another "team" and that feeling of inclusion and loyalty is often difficult to find. When a player has been traded, it normalizes his ego, but really might do a number on his self-esteem.

Learning to accept yourself and striving to ensure you have a healthy self-esteem takes a different amount of time for everyone, and many don't find that contentment until later in life. By that time, you're pretty good about recognizing the difference between ego and self-esteem in other people!

"The very purpose of existence is to reconcile the glowing opinion we hold of ourselves with the appalling things that other people think about us."

QUENTIN CRISP (AUTHOR)

DO YOU LIKE AND LOVE YOURSELF?
DO YOU HAVE SELF-RESPECT?
HOW ARE YOU WORKING ON A HEALTHY SELF-ESTEEM?
HOW DO YOU EXPRESS YOUR EGO POSITIVELY?
ARE YOU ABLE TO LET OTHERS SHINE?

"I believe in education strongly, because I cannot afford the cost of my children not being educated."

BUTCH CARTER

God Bless Teachers

My views on education can be summed up in that single sentence: I believe in education strongly, because I cannot afford the cost of my children not being educated. The teachers and English majors reading this will pick up on that double negative, but you get the point.

If you are not educated, the costs on many levels are great. Some of the tangibles of education are increasing your job opportunities, allowing time to discover talents, and discovering like-minded friendships. Combined with an elevation from poverty, contributions you can make in turn to society and self-development which will last a lifetime, education is truly something that cannot be taken away from you.

This belief in the power and value of education is deeply ingrained in me. My mother always encouraged me to do well in school. I remember coming home to her one day and asking since she was so big on me getting an education, then why wasn't she

educated? I'm sure that hurt her very much, but it also got her thinking.

By the time I got to college and she saw what a productive environment it was for me and how exciting learning was, she went back and got her high school diploma – not at nights, but during the day with all those teenagers (see *The Inspiration of Role Models*). She saw how people could live a different way if they were educated. And, she likes to say she got her Masters degree because it's something Cris and I don't have yet.

Hopefully, everyone can point to at least one memorable teacher who opened the world to them through their words or actions. If I had to pick one person within the system who changed my course, it would be Mrs. Razor, my grade 4 teacher. She sat me down all those years ago and told me she thought I was as smart as the other students in the class. But, my problem was I was trying to fit in and I wasn't taking school seriously. I don't think kids have an easy time at any age, between what they are learning to believe as individuals and in trying to be part of the group.

Mrs. Razor made me understand it was not only permissible to be proud of myself, but how education would prepare me for the future. The kids in this class weren't going to be there 10 years from then so it was permissible for me to compete academically, without worrying about being accepted. She made me understand that being a product of failure was not a life-long curse – if I could be proud of my achievements and my education, that would incrementally make me feel proud of myself.

What I didn't know was that her son had served in the Vietnam War and married a Vietnamese woman, so Mrs. Razor was aware of racism and had to deal with that personally. She gave me the courage to not be ashamed of being smart and gave me a sign that it was acceptable to be the best at something. When we'd get math tests on the board, she said it was fine for me to win it all the time, so that's when I excelled at my

multiplication and division tables. After that, a kid named Brian Campbell was the only one who could beat me in multiplication – but not division.

That special teacher just let me know I was talented and to not accept the norm. I think she and my high school counselor – Bruce Atwater – were the biggest influences on me. He encouraged me to accept education as life-long learning. I spent a lot of time observing what really was going on in life. He helped me understand and refine the game outside the game. He helped me understand why my teammates were passing every week on their eligibility cards but were failing at the end of the year, why they couldn't get their grades, couldn't graduate on time from high school or qualify for their college scholarships. I had to take care of my grades to make sure I didn't end up in the same situation.

One of my great interests has been working with youth and speaking to high school students (see *Community Service*). It's a way that I can give back to a community and promote the value of education and staying in school. Kids are impressionable in their teens. If I can use my stature as a former player and now coach for a terrific NBA team, then if that's what makes them listen to me, I'm happy to get my foot in the door to tell them what I know. I had to learn that I couldn't help them all, but the ones who wanted to be educated could be encouraged. You can't overcome someone who doesn't want to grow from an educational standpoint. Wisdom is only passed on if it's accepted.

I spent a lot of time thinking and was hungry for information. I started reading when I was young. Reading was encouraged in school and I discovered reading was the best way to satisfy my curiosity for the price of a library card. Many boys and young men seem to abandon reading in their teens, but I've never understood that; it's a great cure for boredom, you can go anywhere with a book, and it takes you to places of which you can't even dream. It creates a thirst for more information, and the knowledge gained from reading is invaluable. It also helps you understand the basics – such as fables, classic stories and other

cultures, that playing some computer game will never allow.

Another life-long attribute formalized education provided me with, was excellent study and work habits. I hold things in my mind as if I've taken a picture of them and I also have logbooks and files of all sorts of information. My friends describe me as more or less a walking basketball encyclopedia. Whatever I see, I take a mental picture of it and whatever I talk about, I remember it. I study basketball. I study players. Just like doing homework, I've kept detailed notes of every player, every practice and game, so it helps me make informed decisions later.

Now it's also important for me as a coach to help teach kids about preserving their wealth for later on. This is a good kind of education that I can steer them toward so they can make informed decisions. They may suddenly be making millions of dollars in their twenties, but they have to have a long-term plan in place when they need it, especially if they have a family and children. The most important things for a professional athlete are to save money on a monthly basis, and to use summers to continue to pursue educational goals.

I also spend time looking at the business world outside of sports and using the strategy of what I've learned in one arena by moving knowledge to another. As with a doctor taking art classes, becoming educated in something different re-energizes me and allows me to use a compatible skill set. While it may seem that I need to keep busy to feed my workaholic tendencies, I find it very fulfilling to be involved in business, use emerging technologies and apply strategic business and marketing principles. I graduated with a degree in marketing, so I want to use my knowledge as I grow older and create other opportunities.

No matter what your age, take advantage of educational opportunities. As a father, coach and older brother, I can say that having a formal education is a precious gift you give yourself. Not having an education is a detriment for which you may never know the negative effects until it's too late.

"The best of all things is to learn. Money can be lost or stolen, health and strength may fail, but what you have committed to your mind is yours forever."

LOUIS L'AMOUR (AUTHOR)

WHAT DOES OR WHAT CAN EDUCATION GIVE YOU?
WHAT EDUCATIONAL GOALS DO YOU HAVE?
IS SOMETHING HOLDING YOU BACK?
HOW DO YOU PROMOTE EDUCATION IN OTHER PEOPLE OR
WITHIN YOUR FAMILY?

"We have been worked, now let us learn to work."

BOOKER T. WASHINGTON (EDUCATOR & WRITER)

How Your Environment Shapes You

When I was a kid, I was always at the library and I became interested in biographies. I'd pretty much read about anyone's life. Knowing that a person could make a life for him or herself appealed to me, outside of the circumstances of their family, where they were born or how they were raised.

Many different influences can shape a life; your school, your family, your neighborhood and even your choice of friends. While I wanted a better life, I'm thankful I grew up in the family environment I did as it makes me more compassionate to others and essentially makes me the person I am. I grew up in relatively small towns, with Troy being home to some 20,000 people, and Middletown a working class steel town of 50,000 near Cincinnati, Ohio.

I'm also intensely thankful to my family for creating the best life possible. I've never understood adults who still hold on to the

problems and dwell on their early life; I just think people should get on with life and stop making excuses for what happened to them early in life. There are many people who have overcome so many difficulties and no one would choose to have a difficult start, but no one can re-live life. No matter what you faced as a kid, you can't go back.

Like many young kids, my brother Cris and I felt that a way out of the poverty cycle was professional sports. This is not uncommon and still drives many kids today. Playing professional sports is one way to feel accepted by peers, be respected by others and gain an economic advantage. However, only one percent of all college athletes go on to play professional sports, and it's not getting easier to make it. More are going right from high school and the older players playing longer, so the number of kids who actually make it in pro sports is getting smaller. While education provides opportunities and shows a child's potential, it's easy to see how kids can quickly get turned on to the world in other attractive ways, such as through the media, or entertainment such as music and movies.

Getting involved in sports and learning from your teammates and the coaches is a highly beneficial experience. There is structure, guidance and purpose. Kids can tangibly see the rewards when other kids are recruited, or someone from the neighborhood succeeds. But, even with talent and support, most kids don't make it. The trend to skipping college and going right to the pros from high school deprives them of the time to develop the maturity and adapt to demands of the pros. There's added pressure on them. Maybe they don't feel deserving, can't adjust to the lifestyle changes or continue old behavior. It takes guts and fortitude to construct a new life and seize opportunities when you've been cut down or are hanging out with unhappy peers. Opportunities exist in many ways; professionally and personally.

If you are a child living in poverty, this drive to create a better environment will likely be part of your character. But, with negative influences and temptations, you could fall into drug use

or dealing drugs to make money. Or you could start hanging out with a bad crowd, which will always pull you down. If a kid has no dreams, vision or idea of what's important, then how does he or she know what they want in life?

As I grew, I saw many indications of the possibilities of a better life. For me personally, through my grandparents, I learned committed and joyous love was possible. Through my mother I learned many things, but mostly strength through adversity and that being raised by a single mother can be better for children than maintaining a destructive relationship. I learned that single mothers face discrimination and social stigma. When they had Parent's Night at school there weren't too many kids then with single parents. You could feel it in the air that the teacher thought you couldn't be as good as the other kids. We had to overcome that negativism by personal resolve.

Through my siblings I learned about relationships. And, through my friends and school, I learned there was a better life outside. I grew up in a small town and had a friend, Tom Price, whose family showed me a better way of life, so in turn I could show my brothers and sisters. When I'd go over to his house, there was all sorts of food and nice things around. Tom said I could have a life like that.

Well, it's one thing to tell a kid and another thing to show him. We were friends for five years with a friendship based on people, not color. I liked the way they lived. His dad had a business and his mother stayed home with a housekeeper, and they showed me that I too could have nice surroundings. So, from a relationship as simple as child to child, I could later invite my siblings to see me at Indiana, with an ulterior motive – with my goal being not to just tell them, but to show them the possibilities of a better life.

Through school, kids learn that there are opportunities in the world and many potential ways to contribute. Through travel, the world expands even more and possibilities are really endless. But even with the places I grew up, the cities I played in, and

with the people who influenced me, I'm pretty much the same person all the time. I don't change my personality to suit others or the situation. I see people who are much like chameleons, changing their attributes to suit others or if they feel there will be some personal gain. No matter who it is, I feel conscious of using good manners in how I treat people and how people treat me. I think it's an important thing to try to be nice and respectful to everybody, whether she or he is a cab driver, teller, or a player, because you never know who they are or what hardships they have faced in life.

An example of how a good environment now shapes people is the Air Canada Centre, home of the Toronto Raptors. When we moved into our new facility in February 1999, we were one of the few teams in basketball able to practice and work where we would play. With a practice facility, a full gym with weights, offices and the playing court, we could really count on the feeling of "coming home" when we set out to work. From coming off losses, in two months of games we were almost unbeatable, with 11 wins in 13 games. I think having a great environment was a salient component during that time. We were pumped; the fans felt it too by being so close to us that they could actually see our faces and feel close to the action – unlike baseball or football where fans are back from the action.

"We need a boost from our fans. They've been there for us all year and we can use them again today."

BUTCH CARTER,
APRIL 1999

The fans were terrific from the start. The crowd really is the sixth man out there. In the old facility, the SkyDome, the sound was dissipated because it was such a large building. While home court advantage is always a plus, the Air Canada Centre is intimate and is a big factor in the enjoyment of the game for everyone. When there's a free throw for the other team, the fans are booing and waving signs in their sight line, something you didn't see in the old facility. Vince Carter, 1999 NBA Rookie of the Year, said that we are making the fans love Toronto basketball. He said he's looked into the stands and seen the signs and it's

exciting. We're playing with confidence.

For me, environment is all inter-related. As you grow, your experiences will offer you clues and opportunities to better your environment. By knowing where you come from and what you want in your life, you can create an environment in which you are content. I never forget where I came from.

> *"I lived in libraries. I read everything. That's why I say there's no excuse for a person today to not take advantage of all the opportunities that are available. There is no excuse for ignorance."*
>
> **HAZEL B. GARLAND (JOURNALIST & EDITOR)**

ARE YOU A PRODUCT OF YOUR ENVIRONMENT OR DO YOU CONTROL YOUR ENVIRONMENT?

DOES YOUR ENVIRONMENT MAKE YOU HAPPY AND PRODUCTIVE?

HOW CAN YOU IMPROVE IT?

WHERE WOULD YOU LIKE TO LIVE OR WORK?

"We flatter those we scarcely know,
we please the fleeting guest,
And deal full many a thoughtless blow
to those who love us best."

ELLA WHEELER WILCOX (POET)

The Importance of Family

Our mother and father finally divorced when I was eight, so we moved in with our grandparents. We weren't dirt poor and although there were many bad times, we didn't know any different. My mother did a good job raising us and we made the most of our family situation. Some weeks there was only oatmeal to eat for dinner, and I still can't look at a bowl today. We were also taught to respect ourselves and to haul off into the shower to make sure we were always clean.

Like any family, we've had our own troubles and problems. For me in the early years, I was blessed enough that my grandfather was there to help me through my life.

Although not my given name, when I was born, my grandmother started calling me "Butch" after my cousin Big Butch. As the first born, I had been named after my father, but it was sort of prescient that I was given a new name along the way after a good role model. I was lucky that when I was born, my

grandfather became my buddy. This was in an era when men didn't participate much in the raising of their sons or grandsons but when I was born, he immediately said, "I've got a fishing partner," and was true to his word. I've got pictures of him when I was six or seven months old and he took me out fishing. He could not wait until I started walking.

My grandfather became my best friend. When we went fishing and I'd throw my line up in a tree he never got angry with me or was excitable. When we were fishing we might not get a bite for two or three hours, so I had to learn to be patient and wait, because when your opportunity comes you want to be ready. If you're daydreaming and off throwing stones and a fish bites then you've missed your opportunity. That was a good lesson to learn for later in life. He'd make me practice and gave me a pole and sinker on the line and put an old coffee can in the back driveway. He made me learn how to throw a line underhand, overhand, sidearm, so he taught me technique. He didn't just tell me, he would always explain and never yell at me. He was a calm gentle guy, but very serious about our fishing.

My grandfather and I didn't talk much, but we seemed to understand each other very well. He's the guy I learned patience from and learned to have a sense of humor. My grandmother would make rolls and lay them out to rise when she was at church and grandfather and I would have them baked and eaten before she got home and she'd be furious. He'd go over and hug her and tell her how much he loved her and then he and I would run out the door with our bellies full – laughing. She would bake cakes and leave them out to cool before she'd ice them. Well, we'd have them cut and eaten before she got back in the door.

My grandfather was the one to eventually advise me when I was trying to decide among all the basketball and football schools that were trying to recruit me. He and I were walking around back in the garden and I asked him how come he never said anything about me going to college.

He told me he had an eighth grade education and had been

working in a factory ever since his father died. He had a hard job, but a good job. He made money and was loyal to the company for 35 years. With the college graduates coming in and making as much money in five years as he was just before he retired, he thought I'd better go to college where the athletes went. He just wanted me to graduate from college, he wasn't too concerned about the sports aspect.

I think my grandfather was proud of me, but he had a debilitating stroke right when I started to get proficient in high school, so he could only make it to one game – my very last game of the season. I'm not sure he knew what was going on. He died in 1983 and my grandmother, still desperately grieving and missing her life partner, died a little more than a year later.

I know he did what he could do and I know that he and my grandmother had huge confidence in me and where I'd go. It's as if they took me under their wings, made sure I was launched into the world and waited until I really could fly on my own. They had made me feel special. They had reminded me about the simple things; to treat people nicely and remember my manners. They are the individuals who taught me the importance of giving people confidence in themselves.

Grandparents are very important as they provide a different perspective from parents. Kids need the time and opportunities to absorb their wisdom. I hope to continue the values they taught me through the generations.

I make sure to tell my three sons how much my grandparents meant to me and that they should spend some time with their extended family. I also teach them the values of my grandparents, that I learned long ago. Patience, unconditional love, commitment and respect will always be current to each generation and will never be old-fashioned or out of style.

Apart from Cris, our brothers and sisters are not involved in professional sports. Once I got into pro sports and became a journeyman, my message to Cris was to not follow my path. I said that if he was going to play football, I wanted him to spend

every hour being focused on being a great player. I wanted him to get a contract to provide wealth long past his playing career. I wanted him to be such a renowned player he'd play for one team his whole career. That would give his family some stability instead of moving around the country.

Most of our siblings could be considered successful in their work and lead relatively "normal" lives. My closest sibling in age is a sister who has been there for me every time I needed help and dropped what she was doing – naturally she's developed a nurturing attitude for all of us in being the oldest female child. When we were younger, some of my siblings didn't want to listen to me as the older brother. Some of them thought I was taking life too seriously and they regret and I regret that they didn't understand the power of a good education. I wish they were in a better position to take more advantage of life and enjoy what's going on for all of us.

For me, a blood relation doesn't have much to do with how I see family. A family is only so when they act like family, otherwise they're just taking advantage of your emotions and support. The sad thing is that when you move up the economic ladder – especially from the bottom rung as we did – as bad as you want to, you can't take everybody with you. But, what I decided to do was fund college or a trade education for any family members who cannot pay.

It's very refreshing being in Toronto and seeing the extended families together all the time. They're having picnics in the parks, the grandparents are taking care of the grandchildren and there are first, second and third generations walking together along the boardwalk. When you're on the road, seeing these sights makes you miss your own family even more than you usually do.

"Having family responsibilities and concerns just has to make you a more understanding person."

SANDRA DAY O'CONNOR (JUDGE, US SUPREME COURT)

WHO IS IMPORTANT TO YOU?
HAVE YOU TRIED TO RE-ESTABLISH CONNECTIONS
WITH ANY ESTRANGED FAMILY MEMBERS?
DO YOU HONOR AND HELP FAMILY MEMBERS?
HOW DO YOU STRENGTHEN YOUR FAMILY BONDS NOW?
IS THERE SOMEONE YOU SHOULD PHONE RIGHT NOW?

"I have always told my children that each is unique because only each one can do what they do best. Think of yourself as a hero to your brothers and sisters."

JOYCE CARTER-STAFFORD
(EDUCATOR & MOTHER OF BUTCH CARTER AND CRIS CARTER)

The Inspiration of Role Models

When some people think of role models, they often name someone famous. I don't know how many times I've heard a kid say the current basketball or hockey star was his or her role model. But for me, there's one person who has unfailingly been my role model throughout my life, although I may not have known it at the time: my mother. It may not have been cool to say it when I was a kid, but it's the truth; just as it's likely the truth for most people.

Having seen what my mother endured, her commitment to making the best life possible for her children and having seen what she accomplished in recent years, this all reinforces why I think she's always been the guiding beacon for me.

I grew up as the oldest of seven children and we never saw a father around much, so my mother pretty much held the family together. She was 17 and pregnant with me when she dropped

out of high school and I'm sure she faced many a dark day as she was trying to feed and clothe us and make sure we achieved as much as we could. I can remember I got my football equipment because my mother was cleaning the home of some family who didn't need it anymore. Everything I wore was donated and I said we'd just make the most of it. I knew one day I would be in a position to give something back to my mother and I'm proud I'm able to do so and make her quality of life much better.

She provided the impetus for me to achieve at school and begin college and tried to instill that impetus in my brothers and sisters. Seeing and feeling her pride at my achievements is equal to the pleasure I've felt with any professional goal I've obtained. The knowledge that she takes such pleasure and delight for me has to be one of the most unconditional expressions of love and support there is and I still look to her – although now I look often with pride as well.

For my mother has achieved something very difficult and arduous. After visiting me at college and seeing my academic achievements there, she decided to return to school – at an age when most people had been out working for 20 years! Imagine going to high school after having all those kids and being 15 years older than your classmates. It was not easy. But, she finished and was so inspired by education, she went to college, then went on to get her Master of Education degree and now is a teacher herself.

She is also a terrific role model to struggling families, especially single mothers as they can be shown an example of someone who used to be just like them. I think it was inspiring for my mother to run a daycare center and talk to the mothers who routinely got pregnant and they'd be drawn to her. She'd explain to them how she had all those kids, decided to go back to high school full-time, and how she faced the many burdens. I think it was inspiring as the women could leave their kids with my mother and head off to work or school. She showed them she had lived their lives, she overcame obstacles, and she became successful.

Whenever I hear of multi-million dollar deals, rising stars, overnight sensations and fortune and fame, I still think of how fleeting those achievements can be and I think of the personal accomplishments of ordinary individuals. I believe it's people like my mother who truly quietly guide others and who give our hearts hope. I'm sure I'll never be too proud to say how much I love her.

"A mother is not a person to lean on,
but a person to make leaning unnecessary."

DOROTHY CANFIELD FISHER (AUTHOR)

WHO ARE YOUR ROLE MODELS?
THINK ABOUT THE INFLUENCE OF YOUR PARENTS;
HOW HAVE THEY SHAPED YOUR LIFE?
WHAT INFLUENCE HAVE ROLE MODELS HAD ON YOUR LIFE?
HAVE YOU THANKED YOUR ROLE MODELS?

"The easiest kind of relationship for me is with ten thousand people. The hardest is with one."

JOAN BAEZ (SINGER)

Intimacy

My grandparents were married for 47 years, and when I was young I guess I just assumed that I'd also have a long-standing marriage. I don't think I thought any differently, even though my own parents were not together. Because of the closeness I felt with my grandparents and my constant quiet observation of their devotion, I just thought that their model of a marriage would be what I would enter into. When I did marry at 23, I thought I'd be married for life.

Well, like many marriages, it fell apart. I didn't understand the time I needed to spend with my family to make it work. It does take a lot of work to stay in a committed relationship. Complicating the situation, was my switch from playing to coaching. It was a very traumatic time for us and it wasn't helped by the life on the road. But, there was something fundamental in why our marriage dissolved. We failed to see each other as the primary focus and do anything we could do to preserve that focus.

And, I believe we were partially products of our generation of easy relationships as opposed to my grandparents' time, so the ease of walking away instigated the breakdown of intimacy and trust. Walking away from problems becomes easier than solving them and delaying dealing with issues is a tactful way to avoid dealing with them altogether. Although I regret my marriage failed in longevity, we are raising three wonderful sons and naturally I never regret that. But, it's long past due for both of us to move on and create satisfying and intimate physical and emotional relationships.

However, developing a relationship that can sustain a great intimacy, loyalty and closeness is difficult. In my grandparents' time, people met as part of their community, so often knew the other person from church or a family connection. Relationships developed over time with shared values and beliefs as strong foundations for sustaining love. Friendship and respect deepened to love and faith in the other person, with very little thought of whose individuality was being threatened or compromised. Decisions were made as a team – albeit of two – rather than each person pursuing their individual goals for individual benefit.

I believe the love my grandparents shared is not old-fashioned or out of date. I believe that shared values and beliefs still allow freedom to develop as individuals. I believe a partnership of the soul and body and mind is an unrivaled entity. I still think the idea of essentially giving yourself up for the other person is what it's all about. I believe a committed relationship is ideal; it's a closed unit against the pressures of the world, someone to work out problems with, unconditional support to each other and equals in responsibility.

The idea of courtship and even dating seems almost alien now as people try to develop relationships around time constraints, children, and their professional responsibilities. Even the busy lives people lead now mean a person judges within five minutes whether someone is a potential date, rather than a year of seeing them in your neighborhood.

When you have achieved some measure of success, it doesn't make it any easier to meet people. It's just as difficult to meet someone, except that sometimes I get recognized or well-meaning people are always trying to set me up. In some ways, a person in my situation has a lot to lose, especially if a woman sees me as a meal ticket or expects me to take responsibility for her. It actually makes me weary sometimes and given the pressure, it's a lot easier to just focus on my job. It's hard to find an equal partner and have a "normal" life, but my life is anything but normal and most women wouldn't tolerate my demanding schedule.

Like many people, I worry about growing older and worry about if I can give up all this work to have a life with someone. At the same time, I worry about being alone without work to sustain me. I know people who are passionate about their work, and they get settled into their own routines. It's hard to meld lives when two people have lived on their own and have developed certain ways of living, whether from routine, choice, or just being scared to open themselves to being intimate.

Admittedly, there are also just certain things I don't want to be responsible for in another person's life, nor might they want my "baggage." Still, it boils down to the simplest of desires and partnership. I truly feel you're not going to have a quality relationship unless both parties give up themselves to be with the other person.

I miss all that a loving relationship entails. I miss that feeling of "coming home" with one person. I also miss the small signs of daily affection; of a woman's hand resting on the small of my back as we cross a street, the feeling of a blanket being tucked around me as I take a nap, being brought a cup of coffee unasked or having my neck rubbed when I'm pouring over plays. I also miss doing these small acts of natural affection in return. I still think of the marriage my grandparents had and when I'm 65, I hope to have some of the comfort and unconditional love I saw was so much a constant grounding in my grandfather's life. I just hope I don't have to wait that long to find it.

"Trouble is a part of your life, and if you don't share it you don't give the person who loves you enough chance to love you enough."

DINAH SHORE (ENTERTAINER)

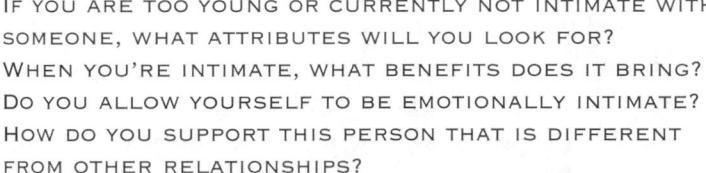

IF YOU ARE TOO YOUNG OR CURRENTLY NOT INTIMATE WITH SOMEONE, WHAT ATTRIBUTES WILL YOU LOOK FOR?
WHEN YOU'RE INTIMATE, WHAT BENEFITS DOES IT BRING?
DO YOU ALLOW YOURSELF TO BE EMOTIONALLY INTIMATE?
HOW DO YOU SUPPORT THIS PERSON THAT IS DIFFERENT FROM OTHER RELATIONSHIPS?
HOW DOES THIS PERSON SUPPORT YOU?

 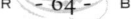

"An athlete retires twice. The first time is when they don't renew your contract. But for a couple of years afterwards you will think you could get in shape and play another season or two. Then one day you look in the mirror and the reality finally sinks in that it's time to find something else to do with the rest of your life."

ARTHUR R. ASHE JR. (ATHLETE & AUTHOR)

Knowing When to Say Goodbye

There are many times in life when you must decide to say goodbye. Perhaps it's a friendship that's deteriorated, a love relationship that is destructive, or a job you despise. While it's admirable to try and work it out, there are just times when you need to let it go. I've had this happen more than a few times in my life and while it is most always difficult, you build up some resilience. I experienced this when I decided to give up playing for coaching, when I said goodbye to my father, and when my marriage ended.

There just comes a time when you know it's over. You know when to let a relationship go. You know when it's time to walk away and end all the grief, the fighting or the mental anguish.

I was married for seven years and we divorced in 1988. We tried reconciliation, but we both really knew it was over. The

years since then have been a difficult balance of sharing care for our children, sorting out visitation schedules, schools and education, phone calls, vacations with the kids and myriad other issues. Unless you have been divorced or ended a long-standing relationship, you can't really imagine the amount of details that you have to sort out to be fair to someone you had loved. There are often parameters to see or speak to your children, and what used to be normal family times – such as meals – are often pressured. It's imperative to ensure your children know of your unwavering love and support for them and for any single parent like me, that is terribly hard to maintain – just from the mere fact you are living in a separate house.

You have to move on to new relationships with a willing heart and all the delight that a new situation brings. You can't do this and give a new relationship the energy or time it deserves if you're still settling problems in the old one. In my case, it's a bit more disjointed as I fly from Toronto and then stay in a hotel to be near my sons. They can't come to my home often as they live and go to school away from me. Plus, as they grow and become young men, they are increasingly developing their own friendships and interests. As much as I try and put them ahead of everything else, living in another city is clearly not our preference.

I know single parenting can work successfully only too well. As a "product" of a single parent home with a father that was never around, I feel that my siblings and I were no worse off than children in a "traditional" home. In fact, I think some one-third of homes with children are now headed by single parents. It's not ideal and I still think a committed marriage is better for raising children, but my children are almost grown – and are wonderful "products" of my ex-wife and I. She's a terrific mother and she does the best she can for our sons, so I know we must have done something right as I can say without conceit that they are great kids.

I don't regret moving on from being a player now – it was a thrilling time of my life. As a player I knew it was time to move

on, but I quit playing before I should have. With a family, I didn't want to bounce around and be a journeyman (traveling around with different teams) and because I was to be traded at the time, for me it was to either go to the new team or quit. I'd done more than I even dreamed of in professional basketball, so I chose to quit. I was only 29 years of age.

In trying to handle my grief, I worked at two jobs, in a financial services company and then with a basketball team. I should have been home more, but as a ball player with a well-honed physical routine, I had to burn off the energy by working as much as possible. I had so much to spare since I didn't have a two or three-hour practice to work it off.

It was important for me to prove I was more than a retired basketball player. I had planned for myself and my family career-wise in what I wanted to do, but I did not understand the pain I had to go through of being out of practice and being away from a team. Although I received a call to go back and play ball, I didn't and I don't regret saying no. In 1986 another opportunity presented itself; I began my coaching career in earnest.

The most important thing about saying goodbye is that in moving around and taking on different roles, I learned to make change easily. I only try to hang on to the things that are good. When things were bad I chalked it up to life's lessons and that's what people need to do – they need to turn loose all the things that are negative and let the things that are good dominate life. You have to learn to move on from disappointment or tragedy. When Pat Riley left the Los Angeles Lakers, it had to be very painful, but he often said he became a better coach by fully closing that door and giving himself fully to his new opportunity.

I find it harder as I get older to say goodbye to people I care about because time is so short. With my family, I make a conscious effort now to say I love them before I hang up the phone or hug them when we leave each other. I just don't know when I'm going to see them next, especially with my schedule. I

hate saying goodbye even in phone conversations – I'd just much rather say 'I'll talk to you later.' I avoid the pain of suspending relationships. Much of that is related to life on the road, as I'd form friendships and leave, form relationships and leave again. It doesn't get any easier, but it preserves time and energy for the life-affirming friendships.

"Phony things can mess up your values…If you start trying to be like other people because of who they are, or who you think they are…you'll end up not being yourself."

GLORIA WADE-GAYLES (AUTHOR)

IS THERE A RELATIONSHIP OR SITUATION YOU NEED TO END?
HAVE YOU SAID "GOODBYE" TO SOMETHING (OR SOMEONE)
AND NOW REGRET IT?
CAN YOU RE-ESTABLISH THE RELATIONSHIP?
IF YOU "SAY GOODBYE" TO A DESTRUCTIVE SITUATION, OR
RELATIONSHIP HOW WILL YOU CREATE SOMETHING POSITIVE?

"Loneliness is the most terrible poverty."

MOTHER TERESA (HUMANITARIAN)

Loneliness

When I'm on a bus in all those different cities going to a game, I look out the window and watch the drivers or people walking about and wonder about their lives. I think everyone observes others – sometimes with envy, sometimes with pity. When you're on the road you can't help but think of the benefits of a "normal" life; given our travel schedules, 24-hour days and one-night stops in different cities.

The things I regret most about being on the road are conversations with good friends face-to-face which don't involve a phone, and missing casual get-togethers such as going to a movie or just for a coffee. I also miss that indescribable feeling of not having to prove myself over and over with friends who are new. I miss laying my head down at night knowing who I am inside is more important to someone than what I do or what I can bring to them. And of course, I miss my family and my sons. This is innate loneliness.

You can be lonely like this as an adult, as a child when no one wants to play with you and as a teenager when friends may make fun of you. Life can be especially difficult when you are young and everyone has difficult times – sometimes you feel as if you will never belong. There are many tragic examples of kids being so lonely or shunned by others that they try to take their own lives or strike out in violence. I don't think I was the only teen who felt lonesome; I think there were maybe only a few people in every high school who rode through the years in a happy breeze while the rest were doubtful, lonely and trying to find their way.

Hopefully, loving parents with other guidance and supports can help you ride out the loneliness. For me, to counteract my loneliness, I relied on my brothers and sisters, my dedication to basketball and my love of reading. But, when you are an adult, it's difficult. Adults are expected to take care of themselves and lift out of funks. Some people can't or won't. There are people who turn to alcohol or become immersed in a personal tragedy so the loneliness just makes the despondency worse. But while a glass of wine or two may make you feel better for an hour, depending on alcohol or drugs to tide you over can be destructive and stop you from taking positive action. Apart from friends who can lift you up and who may get tired of listening to you, there's often little cajoling to keep your spirits up.

Now in my early 40s, building new relationships is difficult. It takes a lot of energy and work, and frankly, I don't have a lot of time given my real job. Love is a risk and intimacy is a risk – you must reveal yourself. It may be news when a public figure can't get a date, but it's not a joke. It's not amusing or rewarding to your self-image to admit that your life would be happier if you were in a relationship. Maybe it's not an advantage, but an upside of being lonely is I can immerse myself more in my job. My passions for ecommerce and reading help me pass the time when I'm lonely. Even on special days, I tend to fall back on work or staying alone, such as on New Year's Eve of the millennium when

I went to bed early and woke up to the fireworks outside the window.

Obviously there is a difference between being lonely and being alone. You can be intensely lonely in a crowd of people or in a room by yourself. I spend a lot of time alone, but when I'm lonely I find the stimulation of keeping active keeps me occupied. While it borders on obsessive, I seem to always have the television on or a video of basketball games on, so I can check out other teams and players. Other days I immerse myself in my office at my home, but I find now I don't like having an office around. It gets to be too much activity and then I'm always busy, always going into the office to do a bit of work, much like people who are self-employed or working at home. You find there is always something to be done that takes you away from having a personal life.

I know there's a perception out there that sports stars are trailed by admirers, road relationships are easy and especially for successful men, there's no shortage of casual women. But the public doesn't hear about the husbands and fathers who are faithful and committed, and who take comfort and pleasure in their families. The public hears about the guys who need to use their status to make women admire them, who don't have the self-esteem to know women want to use them as well. These guys become pathetic jokes about guys who can't sustain a deep intimate partnership. That's just like it is in the rest of the population, maybe like a guy who's always hanging out at a bar and just doesn't want to settle down. I look at the rule, not the exceptions.

These situations may come somewhat easier to athletes — male or female. They're physical people and physical expression and proving athletic prowess daily is how to survive. That may sound elitist but it's just a fact — it may not be right, but when you're a public figure, you're a draw for the opposite sex for all sorts of reasons.

I have good friendships that I've worked hard over the years to keep, and my family and my kids are crucial. When things are

going well, the team is winning and everyone is happy and off celebrating I can't help notice I miss my sons then too. There's actually less work to do in the good times, so I want to share these happy times with them as well as the bad. That's when I miss a strong relationship and my kids most, because everyone wants and needs to share the good times and feel connected to weather the bad times.

To deal with loneliness, I spend a lot of time on the phone talking with friends and try to help others, whether it's talking with a high school coach about a game he's worried about, reading, talking to my family or working on business ideas. If you have a few areas you can concentrate on, or always have a good book on the go, you can get over your loneliness and do something worthwhile to get you through.

"Loneliness is like a spinning wheel
with you controlling the direction.
You may not be able to control the speed,
but you have a say in where it's going."

JOHN A. HALL (SCIENTIST & POET)

DO YOU KNOW THE DIFFERENCE BETWEEN BEING ALONE AND LONELY?
WHAT MAKES YOU FEEL LONELY?
ARE YOU COMFORTABLE WHEN YOU SPEND TIME ALONE?
WHAT PRODUCTIVE ACTIVITIES CAN YOU TURN TO?
WHAT STEPS CAN YOU TAKE TO LESSEN ANY FEELINGS OF LONELINESS?

"You must learn from the mistakes of others. You can't possibly live long enough to make them all yourself."

SAM LEVENSON (COMEDIAN)

Making Mistakes

I learned early in life that if you were a good person and people thought you were genuinely a reflective person, mistakes you made would not always be rubbed in your face if you admitted them, learned from them and moved on. While I don't think I've made too many big mistakes, I still learned from the little ones which steered me on a path. If you're not attentive to the potential damage, the biggest mistake is going down a path not right for you. I see this with kids who get caught up in crime or drugs, or who simply don't believe they can overcome slights against them, a bad start in life or overcome mistakes they have made.

I wasn't always a great student and I did my share of goofing around, which is not something I like to admit now to my three sons, but they can learn from my mistakes. There was pressure on me to do well academically, but like most kids, I thought doing well in school was just something the adults invented to keep the

kids in line. I didn't yet understand the consequences and importance of education. In elementary school, my mother had purposely taken me out of the first class I was in so I wouldn't be able to fool around with my buddies and I could focus on learning.

But then, by the time we moved to Middletown and I was in grade 9, three of my friends and I clowned around the whole time. I wasn't concentrating on my studies and although English was a strong subject, I wasn't doing my homework. With so much going on in the family, and with my three younger brothers and three younger sisters, my mother wasn't able to pay too much attention to what was going on with me. I ended up getting a C in English.

My mother made me haul myself off to summer school for six weeks. So, while everybody was hanging around, playing ball or going to summer camp, I was riding my bike to summer school to take English classes. That was a hard lesson to learn because I didn't want to be in summer school. In our neighborhood, if guys saw you were in summer school they thought you were a dummy, so that was a humbling experience for me. I only had to make that mistake once to learn my lesson to realize that it may not be cool, but it was important to separate myself from something or people who could be detrimental to me over the long run. The buddies weren't going to be with me for life, but my education sure was always going to be part of me.

I also learned to give the bad news to my mother directly rather than letting her hear about it from someone else. She said that she didn't want anyone else getting that little thrill of pleasure out of surprising her with bad news. The first time I was ever cut I remembered that advice, and called a friend in Columbus, Ohio, as I wanted him to go out to the practice field right away where I knew Cris was playing to tell him personally. I didn't want some reporter after the game telling Cris the news. I think this kind of simple communication and courtesy is often hard to practice, but so important in perception.

Little mini-failures are normal parts of growing up, and there were lots of little corrections for me along the way. My values and beliefs made me handle each one with integrity and I learned from my mistakes. I took all those lessons and totaled them up and try to use them every day. Whether missing shots or making scrambled eggs over and over for my brothers and sisters because I burnt so many, it was important for me to just keep trying. I look at showing my sons some new task and remember them as babies and the classic example of them learning to walk. We all forget that we have to start somewhere and will fall down a lot in life, but we need to understand that making mistakes or our frustration is a way of wanting to do better the next time.

That's what young people have to know; things are just going to happen to you and the most important part is to admit your part of the situation that was wrong so you can go forward. While you have to learn lessons, you also need to move on from mistakes. Don't dwell on them. You can't repeat the time. Move on.

> *"When face to face with oneself or looking oneself in the eye, there is no cop out. It is the moment of truth. I cannot lie to me."*
>
> DUKE ELLINGTON
> (MUSICIAN &
> COMPOSER)

For the big failures, I think there also has to be self-evaluation so you can admit that you did do something wrong. Many people meet failures with denial, but that will lead to more failures and lead to more denials and more failures. The cycle is repetitive. All it does is perpetuate a myth that it's someone else's responsibility to clean up the situation. Because I'm a product of a failed marriage and of one man who did not accept the full responsibility of family, and as someone who has had failures, I developed a special way of dealing with setbacks. With my family growing up as a kid, I was in a very nurturing environment to help me deal with failure, so from when I was small, I would refuse to give in to defeat.

I could have made the biggest mistake in my teens, as I think the teenage years are a crossroads for learning how to deal with hazards. I always knew what the parameters were for getting in

trouble. I knew not to take drugs or steal anything – but when that's around you as pretty normal behavior, it's sometimes hard to resist the peer pressure. Succumbing to that peer pressure or coercion is a mistake. While it's probably pretty normal to experiment, it's important to recognize how certain behaviors have the ability to really mess up your life. The mistake is in not listening to your heart tell you it's wrong.

My mother always said failure is temporary and that if I was having a bad day, don't let it become a bad week and don't let it become a bad month. I think that is so valid to remember even now. If I had a setback, made some foul, or was told I'd never be a head coach at a college or the NBA, I just moved on. That type of motivation may have been reverse psychology, but it just propelled me to succeed even more.

One mistake I made when I was a player was when I was with the New York Knicks. The time was great for me as a human being and a father, but bad for me as a professional athlete. In addition, there were a lot of player injuries on the team.

I started to expand myself culturally and began going to events, museums and enjoying the city. As an average player, that's about the worst thing you can do if you want to have a career as my focus was away from playing. My second son was due to be born and my oldest son was preschool age, so we used to hang out in the city. I just passed off the pain of the team losses. It's the most unfocused I'd become as a player and it affected my mental preparation for the game.

A professional sport is a difficult business. It's about failure every game just as much as it's about winning. It's a business where people spend so much time putting down other people with the ultimate goal of winning and being the best. But I've believed, much as I think Cris does, that you can only elevate yourself by elevating others, not by stepping on their backs as you climb. And that's true whether it's in business, life or sports. Just don't let the mistakes weigh you down; correct them and move on up.

"There was a special relationship between my father and Butch. This was not his first grandson either. Butch paved the way for Cris. Every mistake that Butch made in his career, he made sure that his brother didn't."

JOYCE CARTER-STAFFORD (EDUCATOR & MOTHER OF BUTCH CARTER AND CRIS CARTER)

WHAT MISTAKES HAVE YOU MADE THAT STILL WEIGH YOU DOWN?
CAN YOU CORRECT THEM?
IF YOU THINK YOU CAN'T, WHY DO YOU STILL DWELL ON THEM?
HOW CAN YOU AVOID MAKING SIMILAR MISTAKES?

"Good breeding differs, if at all, from high breeding only as it gracefully remembers the rights of others, rather than gracefully insists on its own rights."

THOMAS CARLYLE (AUTHOR)

Manners

Since I've come to work in Canada, I've noticed most Canadians are terribly polite – it has to be the only country where a person apologizes if you step on their toes. I notice good manners, because I was brought up to practice good manners, and to be polite and respectful. Although practicing good manners seemed to be more prevalent in previous generations, good manners have never gone out of style.

I see all sorts of people from all types of backgrounds who have adopted affectations over the years who expect courtesies extended to them, but are ill mannered to others. Having good manners shows consideration of other people, and not behaving as though you alone matter in the world.

Manners include remembering to use the magic words taught when we were young of 'please' and 'thank you.' It includes being an adult and being true to your word, such as saying you'll call that person for the second date when you say

you will, being punctual for meetings, being polite with your elders and patient with the young.

Just as I was taught when I was a boy, my sons have been taught to be polite and respect others. As our sons live with their mother, she takes care in reinforcing their proper behavior almost daily because she makes them practice their manners every day. I was taught to wait my turn in lineups, to be respectful of people older than me, and to be polite and use the "magic words." But manners are more than that, they are a habitual element in civilized conduct and part of our social fabric of interaction. Manners are a form of public language between and among people, that often may be heightened according to a particular social situation, such as if you're hosting a party and aim to make people comfortable. This understanding of appropriate behavior is what makes us considerate and adaptable human beings.

Manners are also connected to public morality and traditions, in that although not law, manners do encourage social communication. This, in fact, equalizes people so that they are each a part of a community as much as another person. Many children and young adults acquire bad manners through replicating what they see adults, their peers or their colleagues do.

Some of these actions can be careless disregard of others and their feelings, or sheer malice. For example, in a work setting where people are in competition for clients, sales or approval from a boss, sometimes manners go right out the window.

We owe it to the children and to society, to instruct how to practice simple standards of good behavior, in efforts to be courteous. This teaches children, intuitively and obviously, that the self-respect they impart to others is expected to be returned to them. If a child does not learn to respect him or herself, he or she may suffer from low self-esteem. Later in life, they may put up with someone being disrespectful, rude or abusive toward them.

Within a family or an intimate relationship, I've never really understood the need to expose a person to public ridicule. I was brought up to believe that in a marriage, what was faced as a

couple was private, for resolution within that unique partnership, so I never understand couples who bicker publicly.

All children are born with an innate sense of justice, so the instruction of manners starts with the parents. Children must be shown when they are young to reciprocate courtesies, to behave politely, to respect each other's rights, and to not hurt each other's feelings or play upon another's weakness. This can be done also by letting older children coach younger children, showing how to apologize and correct slights, and pointing out what qualities to expect from life-long friends and partners.

*"If you want a person's faults, go to those who love him.
They will not tell you, but they know."*

ROBERT LOUIS STEVENSON (AUTHOR)

DO YOU PRACTICE GOOD MANNERS?
HOW DO YOU HELP TO INSTILL RESPECT FOR OTHERS?
WHAT CAN YOU DO TO PRACTICE GOOD MANNERS NOW?

"Many people devote their entire lives to the pursuit of greater ease and pleasure. Those who have not found the 'why' that gives meaning to existence may achieve material success, yet the real goodness of life eludes them. One true meaning of life lies in sharing our particular qualities of greatness with others."

SIR JOHN TEMPLETON (FINANCIAL FOUNDATION & AUTHOR)

Mentoring

Whether in business, sports or school, everyone does better with a mentor: someone who knows the ropes and can guide you through problems or challenges with advice, wisdom, motivation and a good reality check. I had various mentors growing up and I still learn from people all the time, but I never had a formalized arrangement. As a coach, I try to use this informal model between the younger and veteran players and find that works well on many levels.

First, it helps provide the younger players with a sense of balance. They understand pretty quickly that they must be part of a team environment, no matter how much everyone or the media says someone is the new rising star. With this reality check early from an older player, a younger one can concentrate on improving his skills and drills with someone who has his best interests at heart. Second, it helps give the older players a sense of responsibility of giving back; of helping other players develop the

skills maybe they were taught by others – and they also benefit with the enthusiasm and energy the younger ones exhibit. So both groups get something tangible and intangible from the arrangement. When a couple of players mesh or really help one another through tough times, that's another natural sign of someone who's there ready to help.

Now, this situation is true no matter if it's sports, being a buddy in a school program, or a business mentor. A good mentor understands a person's strengths and weaknesses and doesn't jump in to correct problems – but does guide you to overcoming problems and developing your potential. If you get to a point where you just can't make a decision, they give you the perspective because they know what path you should take. It's often close to a parental, sibling or coach relationship but many guys don't even sound their fathers out when they get to a fork in the road as there's sometimes no perspective, an intimidation or limited experience with an issue. It's common even in the business world now to use the word "coach" rather than mentor because "coach" has a more positive perception of coaching the person through an issue rather than directing it.

I also became more aware of specific team talents, such as the importance of acquiring playoff-type rebounders. Although I struggle with not having a mentor now, I do look to top-notch coaches. Although mentoring tends to be a personal experience, these lessons are also learned publicly. I learned the value of how to organize statistics, that the season is not one long journey, it becomes short trips by organizing games into sets. I also was taught a good lesson privately for when I would become a coach. Rather than being cut by a head coach, I was once by an assistant coach, so from then on, I vowed if I ever had to cut anyone, I'd do it myself.

The coach I admire most is Pat Riley of the Miami Heat, because he was the first to show how a former player could work so terrifically hard, could understand the variables and nuances of coaching and show how to motivate the highest level of athletes.

Nothing was guaranteed to him, he had to fight for every dollar and there was huge resentment between various non-playing coaches and playing coaches. Non-playing coaches wanted to keep their jobs and prove the guys who played couldn't translate their skills to coaching. And many players who did try coaching couldn't handle it – they were used to going to a two-hour practice and be done. Well, the day just starts when you're a coach as you're reviewing videos, doing interviews, or meeting with assistant coaches. Pat set an example for me. What I respect most about him is his work ethic. He understood every summer he still had to prove himself as a coach. While the others were thinking they were going to run the same plays, the same defense and same offense, he was not coming back as the same coach, so his players weren't coming back to be the same players. This example makes me a better analytical coach and encourages me to be critical of myself.

I try to show the players in every manner how they should conduct their business and find out what specific help they may need, to help them become competent in other areas. My role is actually similar to being the chairman of a company and these guys are my board of directors. If you have members of a board who are all millionaires, you can't tell them they are stupid and rant and rave – you have to step back and bring them along. I've got to guide the company and balance all the interests. What I've learned with the young guys is that I've got to spend some time at their level to understand what they need and where they need guidance.

"He (Butch Carter) took time out to find the best person and best situation for me to feel comfortable with. You don't have too many coaches in the league who care that much about their players."

TRACY MCGRADY
(PLAYER, TORONTO
RAPTORS)

I've seen so many teams fail when they turn their locker room over to the younger guys. Our younger guys aren't allowed to make any decisions – their concern is to be the best basketball player they can be individually. As a player, you have a different perspective than as a coach. As a coach, you have to filter what a

guy is telling you; whether it's for the sake of the team or his own personal turf. So, I seek out the advice of the older players.

I knew Charles Oakley had helped a great organization – the New York Knicks – and when he came to the Toronto Raptors I decided to use him as a resource; such as getting his opinion on where we needed help. I even think the reason Oak stayed with us in renewing his contract for the 99/00 season is because of his strong relationship with Vince Carter. You don't have to worry about much with Oak because he's for the team and his teammates. He likes the rules and he likes that he doesn't have to be a cop or a babysitter for the younger players. But he's a natural mentor in his professionalism and how he shows a tough side of playing, for example when he sacrifices his body taking charges and diving for balls.

On the other hand, when you take a skillful younger player such as Tracy McGrady, there's talent that can only flourish within a mentoring environment.

No matter what your field or skill level, I think mentoring is very helpful when you're deciding on a career path or wanting to open your own business. You have to almost let people see and taste the value of mentoring in a passionate way to help launch a dream.

Some of the tips I found helpful are to look for a mentor who loves what he or she is doing and is passionate about passing on that knowledge. It helps enormously if there is good chemistry between the two of you, as a mentor doesn't always tell you what you want to know, but what you should consider, so both parties need to have a healthy personal respect. As well, you should be interested in your mentor and ensure there are ways you can give thanks or honor his or her role in your life. Of course, you will want to parlay that mentoring relationship into one of your own and help others.

"Butch had been preparing to be a great coach his entire life. He brought his strength of character and vision to the Toronto Raptors and in doing so, has molded this young team into being serious competitors. He believed in them and in turn, they have believed in themselves."

RICHARD A. PEDDIE (PRESIDENT & CEO, MAPLE LEAF SPORTS & ENTERTAINMENT LTD.)

HOW HAS SOMEONE BEEN A MENTOR TO YOU?
IN WHAT SPECIFIC GOALS OR SKILLS DID THEY HELP YOU?
COULD YOU USE ANOTHER MENTOR IN YOUR LIFE NOW?
WHAT CAN YOU PROVIDE AS A MENTOR TO GIVE BACK TO AN
INDIVIDUAL IN YOUR COMMUNITY?

*"I don't think black or white, I think of human beings.
My mother raised me that way."*

SARAH VAUGHAN (SINGER)

Racism

Can you tell by looking at a person what his or her beliefs are? If you need a blood transfusion during surgery, do you care about the person's color, gender or religion?

Can you determine what's in a person's mind, background or the goodness of his or her actions by the color of their skin or their age? Well if you can, you're an anomaly. I can't and one thing I do know categorically is that you cannot assume anything about a person's belief system just by looking at them.

How do people come to believe that others are the enemy, are "stealing" jobs only they are entitled to, or living in communities they should not? It's ignorance, a lack of understanding of other people and cultures, ageism, chauvinism or racism; all those pre-conceived misconceptions we can often be taught as we grow up. It reflects the human race trying to control resources they think are God-given or their birthright.

I don't think racism is just color-based. It is also apparent in

Ireland with the Protestants and Catholics. It's among the Serbs, Croats and Muslims. It's with the Jews and foreign workers in Germany. It's present among the Chinese, Vietnamese and Koreans. I had not studied cultural imperialism or the history of oppression in the world much in school; the only environment I knew was Troy, Ohio. All I knew then was some color-based racism.

In Middletown, Ohio, where we moved to after Troy, there was *de facto* segregation – meaning, lines were drawn by housing and the proverbial going across the tracks. In high school basketball, we knew only so many blacks would be allowed to start the game, perhaps three players. We had just moved into the community, so I was supposed to be the fourth starter.

My mother was in the concession stand lineup, behind the mother of a player who was complaining about me moving to town as a starter, and she and her husband were not going to put up with it. I scored 20 points that first game, but I never got to start a game for the rest of the year, even though I was the team's second highest scorer that year. One player they replaced me with was the son of a local radio announcer. He didn't go on to college on a basketball scholarship, but he was classified as good enough to play in the starting lineup. This was very painful to me, but I made up my mind I was going to be so good the next year, they'd have no choice but to start me.

It wasn't oppression to me though, as once I figure out where someone stands, I figure out a way of getting around. Every time some obstacle like that came up I just worked harder. If you are willing to accept the way things are – for whatever reason – you have very little chance to work to change it. I just lived, ate and drank basketball and I ended up being one of the top two players in the state.

It was still that kind of old-boy environment and informal quota system until I became the head coach back in Middletown. I was the first non-white coach and as of the 99/00 season, was still the only non-white who coached there. We were the high

school program with the most wins in the whole state and a lot of talent came out of that little steel town. I went after the high-energy kids who would match my energy, and if I wanted to practice twice a day, these were the kids who would say "let's go." They were trying to find excuses to get into the gym instead of getting out of the gym and I liked their attitude. That success, and the fact the fan seats were filled, is something people probably thought would never happen in town.

Although I had always been respectful of others, no matter what color of skin or religion, gender or age, it was after my experiences traveling throughout Europe as a young man when I learned there were different forms and permutations of racism. I was 19 years old in 1979, and in Europe my first time, for three weeks on a basketball tour. I was in four countries behind the former Iron Curtain and I got to see communism first-hand. I think all of us on that tour had taken for granted the simple benefits available to us at home and learned to appreciate them.

My first experience with racism other than color-based was when a restaurant owner in France screamed insults at our bus driver, who was Arab. Ethnic and religion-based racism was new to me, and continuing to travel is how I educated myself – by seeing different races and their experiences. I was able to understand the books I had read when I was younger about the explorers, the discovery of countries and people; all these things were now larger than in any book.

I became sensitized to other forms of racism more after visiting northern Africa. I went to Kenya where one tribe doesn't like another tribe – which surprised me because they were all the same color. And I learned no matter your race, people even of your own color or faith will fool you into the faulty idea of loyalty in that 'we've got to stick together.' Regardless of color or faith, I think you have to be loyal to the people who gave you an opportunity.

For me, I found the sheer opportunity of coaching in Toronto really restored my faith in my beliefs. I honestly don't

think the owners of my team gave it a second thought that I am black. They let Glen Grunwald hire me, probably not knowing that it's rare for a black coach to be hired after a black coach has been fired. I don't think I had any strikes against me walking in. They took what I could do at face value and the only issue was of whether I was capable of getting the job done – not the color of my face.

The owners are hard working people and have either started or taken over family businesses and taken these businesses to another level. They wanted a worker. They set good standards – regardless of race or religion. I was going in to work at 6:30 in the morning but I was still half an hour behind them. My contract extension to continue to coach this team has a far greater value to me than any monetary payment; it's a sign of acceptance and skill and has got nothing to do with color. It's a sign of their belief in my skill. It's got to do with work style, reputation and dedication; all those things my job should be based on, instead of finding a reason the guy can't get the job done unrelated to the actual job.

I don't care anything about the color of my skin in coaching; if I fail, then I've failed as a coach, not as a black man. I want to beat Lenny Wilkins and Phil Jackson as a coach, not because they are white. I want to beat them because they are great coaches. I don't want to use the excuse that because I'm black I can't compete against them.

It's fact there is a discrepancy in the ratio of black coaches to players and there are even some racist coaches still today, who debase other coaches or disrespect their peers, some of whom happen to be black. This is not carping; it's unfortunately still prevalent.

Adults perpetuate a lot of the attitudes, whether through ignorance, hatred or fear. Kids model what they see and how others act, so if they hear subtle racist comments or overt actions, they'll think those are acceptable ways of behavior. It's sad and destructive when one generation is not working to build up the next, but in fact tearing it down to the detriment of the next

generation. I think the main point is bad behavior is just that; there are white yahoos and there are black yahoos, and there are jerks of every color and either gender.

That unfortunately includes people in leadership positions who should know better. One item reported in the media noted how a baseball coach, who is white, was making racist remarks publicly when a black man expressed his concern. A scuffle ensued, it became an incident of public record, yet the coach is still coaching, with people accepting that this incident is just part of his character. What is surprising is the lack of remorse, lack of understanding of the deep hurt he creates and what this illustrates as someone who is in a position of leadership.

Cris and I each have leadership qualities as strengths and being black, I think there is a greater responsibility for us to try to be respected leaders. If I let color-based racism dominate my thinking, I could just use that as an excuse not to do anything. But, there still are tangible signs. I was asked once if I had really used the word "impetus" in a media interview, or if the reporter had written it. I just had to shake my head. That's what blacks have to face all the time – the subtle racism of perhaps a black man wouldn't be educated enough to use certain words.

There's a correlation to women in the work world; they have to rise above the male norm. When you are different from the norm in any way, you can't afford to be mediocre. You always have to be a bit better dressed, better spoken, stronger, a greater athlete, superior coach, excellent student or driven businessperson to be taken seriously – or even to be accepted as an equal. And, even then you have to be modest and not use ego to lord it over someone or you may be seen as snobby or undeserving. It's a vicious cycle and there is no way to win except to live your life for you and do the best you can within your resources.

Canada has allowed and offered so many opportunities for people of color, compared to the United States and many other countries. In being a cultural melting pot, Canada has truly been a land of opportunity. I explained to Glen early on that I've never

been happier than I've been here in Toronto, because – and this is nothing to do with the team – people are nice. That may sound kind of insipid, but it's a great attribute. Canadians are nice; there is hardly any crime, there is great respect, sincere politeness and genuine support.

I talk to my sons about racism and the truth is they don't expect it – it's my reality and not theirs. I don't think it's right for me to poison them with my experiences. I say that my thoughts are not your thoughts and you are not me. I think that you get cycles and what happens is that one generation beats the next one down with everything that's bad that happened to them. Some people say, "you're not going to be able to do this" and "you're not going to be able to go there," so that immediately sets up some fences that shouldn't be there. The most important thing I've done with the boys, since they were very small, is I've always asked them to tell me their names. I get them to yell their names as I want them to feel pride in knowing exactly who they are. I intend to take them to Europe to visit some of the countries and not just tell them what I experienced, I have to show them a life outside of their world.

I think the main thing to understand is everyone is likely going to face some type of disadvantage whether it be color, social, or religious, so you have to find some way to persevere, no matter the reason. The biggest advantage of dealing with the ignorance of prejudice is not letting them know you know what's going on – because if you let them know they'll just find a better way to hide what they really think, which perpetuates the problem.

I, Too, Sing America
Langston Hughes

I, too, sing America.

I am the darker brother.
They send me to eat in the kitchen
When company comes
But I laugh,
And eat well,
And grow strong.

Tomorrow,
I'll be at the table
When company comes.
Nobody'll dare
Say to me,
"Eat in the kitchen,"
Then.

Besides,
They'll see how beautiful I am
And be ashamed –

I, too, am America.

*"I saw I could do a helluva lot more for Blacks by
being a Black artist rather than a Black activist."*

PAUL WINFIELD (ACTOR)

DO YOU TRY TO MAKE PEOPLE FEEL ACCEPTED AND EQUAL?
DO YOU HAVE PRECONCEIVED NOTIONS OF PEOPLE BASED ON
COLOR, RELIGION, AGE OR GENDER?
DO YOU KNOW WHY?
HOW CAN YOU TRY TO ELIMINATE THESE DETRIMENTAL NOTIONS?

"I think it's a well-known fact around the NBA that the Raptors are for real. They've done an extraordinary job in bringing in the right players and developing the team. Butch is a no-nonsense type of guy and he's got them playing aggressive, smart and tough, and I think their record is indicative of that."

PAT RILEY (HEAD COACH, MIAMI HEAT)

The Responsibility of Leadership

Being a coach is who I am – it's always been part of me as the oldest child and the older brother; the responsible person. While it may create havoc in my personal life, that caretaking role is a great position to come from if you want to coach. I think my purpose in life was decided early and was decreed by the birth order and guiding role I played in my family. Although it was very hard on my siblings, I decided early that if I was going down a path with six people, I wanted to be first no matter what.

One of my skills is that I often see what the player doesn't; I can connect what they are doing in relation to the others, in a broader sense of where and how they fit in to the team environment. Coaching is easy compared to life's challenges because there are far fewer variables. Coaching is predictable because I know what's going to happen. Normally with an athlete

there is only one of two ways they're going to react – good or bad. The most dangerous people I've been around are people who say they don't care. It's one of the first signs they disrespect themselves and see themselves as powerless to change a situation. To ensure good player relationships, I need to address problems beforehand, be self-disciplined to not let issues slide, otherwise I'd always be in reaction mode. I've got to be a beam of light for them (and not the light at the end on the approaching train). I'm also not a screamer or into public histrionics, as the Toronto fans well know. I try and keep emotion-based reaction inside.

It took a few hard lessons in learning how to control my emotions. When I was 12, Cris and I were in a playground and he fell off a swing and sliced open his head. I immediately sprinted and ran a couple of miles to get the adults, but realized afterward that it was the wrong thing to do – I should have taken care of Cris immediately. He was fine with some stitches, but I still remember it as if it was yesterday, as I thought I didn't handle it well. I was just a kid and did the best I knew how to at the time, but since then, realized there are different ways to handle things, and it taught me to think out situations. The other lesson was that if you are hard on yourself, it's easier than someone else being hard on you.

People have a difficult time with that as before they get a chance to say I've screwed up, I've usually admitted to it and it becomes part of being accepted and respected. I'll try not to screw up the next time and I can change something once I've accepted my part in the problem. An example of that was the opening game of the 99/00 season when we lost to the Boston Celtics and Rick Pitino (the night I call the Boston Massacre). I was upfront with the players, the media and everyone who called me predicting doomsday, saying I'd get it straightened out. I felt it was my responsibility to fix. If I didn't admit to what happened so we could move on, I don't think we could have come back and won three games straight. I don't think we'd have had a chance. I think that's good leadership.

I don't care whether I'm right as a coach, I want to be right as a man. A coach, gave up on Cris all those years ago, because he wanted to be right and Cris had the guts to come back with a coach at the Minnesota Vikings who saw he was ready to work. And I won't give up on someone if he's ready to work. That's good leadership.

Good leadership is also doing something unexpected in your own style, and taking responsibility for creating a mood. An example is one time in the 98/99 season when the team had been going through a tough time but was working really hard. I'd given the players a huge speech the day before a game about how I needed all of them to give up something and find the passion and love for basketball that they had as a kid. I know they thought I was crazy, as it wasn't about practicing – we just needed to get that passion back so what I was trying to do was bring them together with emotion.

We lost the game with the Charlotte Hornets on the last shot made by Derrick Coleman so I wanted to make them practice twice the next day. I stomped on the bus as if we were going to practice and it was pretty glum. You could have heard the proverbial pin drop it was so quiet. But, I had called around that morning to see if we could get a whole movie theatre. So the bus pulls up and we filed out. The older guys knew right away what I was trying to do and bought in, when they could have decided otherwise.

I had also arranged for limousines for all of them to go out after for dinner. I had the older guys organize where the younger ones would go and sent one of the married guys off to dinner with his wife who was in town. Mentally there was nothing we could have accomplished in practice that day and I knew we needed a mental break from the pressure. We practiced the next day, they worked hard and we had a great day.

Part of what I need to do as a coach and a leader is to treat the players like men working toward a common goal, but some coaches still aim to treat players as kids to be reigned in. When a

skilled player such as Tracy McGrady reflects on this time when he's older, and can say that I treated him like a man and I helped him grow, then I'm happy. I get more from them in watching them grow and develop in their own ways, rather than getting them to adopt to a rigid style.

I'm not a traditional coach in that I don't always prescribe what to do and how to do it – in the pros now you will have better players on your team who have worked with great coaches and that can be a big pitfall if you disrespect their knowledge. If you cull the knowledge that a player knows, question him fairly, and filter out what's for personal gain, you then can't turn around and tell that player to be quiet. I believe that young players have to prove themselves with deeds, not words. Part of my leadership is to help a player obtain what he wants personally, but not at the expense of the team.

Leadership doesn't mean you can be a dictator, especially with the well-respected veteran players. Although respect should not be based on money, almost every guy on the team is making more money than I am. So if I went to dinner with the guys, there is a certain amount of respect going back and forth across the table anyway. Am I not supposed to give that respect back because the guy is a basketball player on my team? I give it freely and I demand it back.

And, if we're going to argue I want us to argue together – not as family but as men. What I have to do is to earn their respect so when it's time for me to push them they'll support me pushing them. We want to be aggressive and tough and be able to go out and not be scared to go after the win. I'm being paid money to keep control and keep the team organized and positive and I have to understand what motivates each of the players.

As interim coach in 98/99 and then head coach, I took over leading the team during a six-month lockout, a shortened season and only two exhibition games to get us ready. We had a turnaround year and I think that's due to the fact of good leadership from our veteran players and coaches who expect the

best out of the players all the time.

One stellar example of leadership exists within our own club; Glen Grunwald, who's been with the Toronto Raptors since 1994 as a Vice President. When Glen took over as General Manager in 1997 as the one person brave enough to lead the club, the team finished that season with a terrible record – a franchise worst – of 16 wins and 66 losses. Glen soothed detractors and acknowledged the boos of fans by taking the microphone at a game in April 1998, diffusing emotion by telling fans he understood them. The team was admittedly a complete mess, with direction and control evaporating. Leadership and stewardship became the most important task of rebuilding the club. If you remember reading the classic book *The Lord of the Flies* by William Golding, you understand how a lack of leadership can be so destructive.

Known in the league for doing a great job in rehabilitating a club known as a disaster, orchestrating great trades and free agents to round out the team, Glen does this all without berating anyone, throwing his weight around or with a shred of a mean streak or ego. While Glen may have felt the only place to go with the team was up, it's a testament to his calm style of leadership in that a year later, the team was making a playoff berth bid.

Reinforcement of Glen's leadership ability was a strong management message from the executive team, since the stability and cohesiveness of the Toronto Raptors might be eroded if we all had to be worried about our secure leadership continuing. The team could then relax in knowing this stewardship was reliable and resolute – with understated implication that hard work would be rewarded without histrionics or demands.

Much attention is given to the players and there's a microscope on the coaches, but it's the whole leadership structure which actually gives any team a foundation.

"Butch is a coach who subscribes to the golden rule. He treats our players with respect and he is respected by our players. At Indiana (University), Butch received more of the pressure and responsibility from Coach Knight than did other players. Because of that additional responsibility, Butch can now deal with stress and criticism better than a lot of other people in the NBA. Those tough times at Indiana made him a better coach and leader."

GLEN GRUNWALD (GENERAL MANAGER, TORONTO RAPTORS)

HOW ARE LEADERSHIP SKILLS IMPORTANT TO YOU?
DO YOU GET THE OPPORTUNITY TO USE THESE SKILLS?
CAN YOU LEAD A WORK TEAM, SCHOOL PROJECT, OR
VOLUNTEER GROUP FOR ADDED EXPERIENCE?
WHAT LEADERSHIP SKILLS DO YOU NEED TO ACQUIRE?

"I don't ever want my children to look at me and think that I wilted like a daisy over stuff. When you risk, you aren't always going to succeed. But to me, real heroes are men who fall and fail and are flawed, but win out in the end because they've stayed true to their ideals and beliefs and commitments."

KEVIN COSTNER (ACTOR & DIRECTOR)

Taking Risks

I admire people who take calculated risks in pursuit of goals in search for a better life. How could someone not respect that? But there are people who do not, and will try to prevent a person from taking a chance to improve their life. I think that's because of the destruction or disintegration of her or his own goals. If a young girl says she wants to be an astronaut, just who is that hard-hearted person to scoff at her or ridicule her? If a young boy says he wants to be a nurse, encourage him. It's a risk even stepping out of the norm, but all sorts of people are needed to grow up to be the astronauts or actors, teachers or doctors.

There are many types of risks in life, but the worst is to not take the risk of improving yourself. Determining what – or who – you want in your life can be a huge risk, but if you avoid the risk of improving yourself, you certainly will be dragged down. At any time of life there is a risk of getting involved with a bad crowd, or feeling the peer pressure to do things you don't really

want to do. Sometimes you must risk going against the group to find your way.

You have to turn negatives into positives, otherwise the bad things just pile up and bury you – it is so important to know that the decisions you make sometimes can punish you for the rest of your life. The point is to be true to what you know inside, to take the best route for you and to not expect an easy way out.

I never really considered doing anything else than playing basketball – I never knew anything else. Although I was good at whatever sports I tried, playing basketball was something everyone did and it was easy. We lived in a small neighborhood and went to a community center, played basketball and went swimming, so I think that early athletic ability and activity was helpful to keep me occupied and out of trouble. The guys in my neighborhood all played and it was expected as kids that you get into sports anyway.

I also took a huge risk in choosing Indiana as I was going to school out of state. When you're an in-state athlete you have a natural advantage as normally coaches are going to play you as much as possible because it's recruiting territory. It's also a hometown crowd so the local players will drive attendance. It's all part of the business aspect of sports. But I made my decision based on the best college for me and not the basketball. So I made the decision at 16 and left at 17 years old.

Although it was a risk moving from playing to coaching, I'm now glad I made the move when I did, although it was hard at the time.

As I've gotten older, there are not too many risks I take with my life, thoughts or feelings. Most of what I do is fairly controlled, predictable and revolves around basketball. That's just my character and my background. I understood what I needed to do long ago to achieve what I wanted, and from the standpoint of my training, I turned a perceived negative into a positive.

For the team, people may have thought it was a risk having an NBA team in Toronto, but I thought if you had the fourth largest

city in North America you should eventually have the ability to be at least one of the four best teams in the Eastern Conference. I knew if we'd get the right players up here they'd be socially happier than in the US because Canada is a different environment.

Although many motivational people and books will tell you to seize the day and take a risk, I've done pretty well by following a path of hard work and calculated action, taking small risks along the way. We tend to hear about the big risks people take; mortgaging houses to start a business, selling all possessions to tour the world. But, calculated methodical risks are just as challenging, whether it's risking capital in the business world, picking a school or starting a new job. We just don't hear about the daily type of risks we all take. I don't think anyone could call me a showy risk-taker, but no matter what, I've stayed true to my beliefs.

> *"He who is not courageous enough to take risks will accomplish nothing in life."*
>
> MUHAMMAD ALI (ATHLETE)

WHAT CALCULATED RISKS HAVE YOU TAKEN?
IN AFTERTHOUGHT, WHAT BAD RISKS HAVE YOU TAKEN?
WHAT PROFESSIONAL RISK WOULD YOU LIKE TO TAKE?
IS THERE A PERSONAL RISK YOU WANT TO TAKE BUT ARE AFRAID OF BEING RIDICULED?

"The joys of parents are secret, and so are their griefs and fears."

FRANCIS BACON (PHILOSOPHER)

What Children Bring To Your Life

Whatever else is going on with my life – both the good times and the bad – having children is truly what keeps me grounded. When we first married, I wanted to wait to have kids and my wife wanted them right away. I couldn't argue that we could not afford having children, as I was just starting out in my pro career so there was some expectation of financial security.

However, the truth is, I was afraid I'd be away from them too much in the early years being on the road, missing much of their daily lives in growing up, and being of little help to my wife with me having to travel. We had three sons and my concerns all turned out to be true. Still I don't regret it, as what gives me intense joy is watching my sons grow up the way I've almost dreamed about and knowing they are well-mannered, intelligent, and socially adjusted. Their mother has done a great job helping

them learn to make good decisions and the credit goes to her for taking care of them. She was really born to be a good mother.

I am incredibly conscious of preparing a better world for children. I look at what I must do to launch the lives of my sons, as well as knowing the words and lessons I can pass on. That's what it was like explaining life to my younger brothers and sisters, and is much like being a coach.

I think only a parent really understands how precious and fleeting that feeling is of a child's hand holding yours when you cross the street, cupping a tiny foot in your palm, or lifting a child into your arms for a loving hug. It's not the overtime points, a great salary or being admired by thousands that is important in life – it's the ability to look into a child's eyes and to be able to understand the whole world's purpose within the tiny miracle of a new person. This may not sound profound or manly. But, I think if more men put their egos aside and acknowledged their responsibility to their children and took the time with their kids that they do in trying to own the world, create wars or run a company, the world really would be a better place. Similarly if more men got up from a meeting at work and said they had to leave to go pick up their child from school, that would go a long way in the working world to reiterate the importance of a child's life.

Kids used to spend more time in neighborhood groups and not driving for miles to meet friends. I rode my bike right up until high school and played sports with the same teams. While exposure to other communities and people is good, the flip side is kids are now being driven to school or practices, so it takes them out of their community. Kids can also become more prone to random pressures and transient activities of the new kids, rather than having to get along with kids all the time in their community in everyday dealings or meeting their parents.

I am desperately thankful my mother provided the stability

in the lives of my siblings and me where my father did not. I think that's why I feel such a responsibility to ensure my sons are provided for spiritually, mentally, emotionally and financially. I am highly conscious of what I can do to give them as "normal" a life as possible, being a supportive father. It's important for them and for my family to have distinct relationships with them. For example, it's crucial for them to develop relationships with Cris and my other brothers and sisters, because if they are having trouble in life or not doing something they're supposed to do, we need someone to be able to reach them emotionally who may not be a parent.

I've seen a lot of athletes' kids brought up in the environment of professional basketball and while it brings rewards, I know it's not a normal life. They see the fancy cars and easy lifestyle. The parents give them everything and the kids think it's always going to be like that. I have some basic rules for my kids. My kids don't usually go to NBA games and because most locker rooms are unfit for any kids to be in, I don't let them in. It's an unreal world. It's also important that kids learn to like a team rather than revere an individual player.

And unlike some fathers, I don't want my sons to replicate my life. I know some want their sons to recreate their life or do what they have not achieved. I try to encourage their skills without turning them into sports nuts. My sons have been brought up away from sports and although they play for fun, I want them to have a normal life. My sons are a huge relief to me and they also take me down a notch. They also make me less serious and make me less aware of being me. For those who really know me, that's quite an achievement.

The boys also make me laugh and I live a lot of my life through them. They're not encumbered by responsibilities yet and they get a chance to be kids rather than grow up before they're ready. The things they do are hilarious compared to the antics of my three brothers and me. For instance, my middle son and I went to play golf and on the way back he pulled out my

laptop computer and created a slide presentation of our day of golf. I've saved it for him to remind him years from now just how much he made me laugh and to feel connected to him.

I look at my sons both individually and as a group, in that they are both the next generation and they are individual people. I also consciously make the effort to have personal time with them and I go on a trip with each of them separately when I can. That became a lot harder taking on the project of the basketball team and the summer of 1999 was the first year I wasn't able to take a vacation with each of the boys. That's a price I have to pay as they become older. I also go away with the three of them together and during basketball season they normally take a road trip with me. That time gives us 24 hours, seven days a week of bonding and having a good time. In the lockout of the 98/99 season, I was on a plane every weekend to be with them, staying in a hotel, returning to the office Monday morning.

One of the simple ways I discovered to listen better to my children was to turn the radio off when I'm at home or in the car. It forces me to be communicative and really hear what they're talking about. When the radio is off, I listen to them and they to me; although they may not acknowledge that. In today's society we spend so much time in the car going to the movies, taking kids to sports practices, or to school and it's easy to spend a couple of hours daily in the car. If I turn the radio off, I can take mental notes of what kind of moods they're in or if they're having good or bad days. And to resist the outside world, I rarely take my phone with me. I used to be able to talk to my sons daily, but being divorced, there are restrictions.

I was always a big reader when I was young and now my oldest son and I exchange book recommendations. It started when he was reading a book in junior English class and I didn't like the material. So, I gave him a book I wanted him to read and told him to pick a book for me. He gave me *Their Eyes Were Watching God* by Zola Neale Hurston and I remember telling him I found it a difficult read. It was written in the Southern

vernacular, in 1937 by a woman who faced hardship, but found her spirit. Although I had to work to stick with it, I found the meaning memorable and was so very proud my son had culled its messages. Another book we discussed was *A Lesson Before Dying* by Ernest J. Gaines; an incredibly moving novel about dignity that can give life to even the most dry heart. I've found this to have been a great way to keep track of what's going on in this son's life, albeit a small way.

My oldest son is now at the point of deciding on college and I would love to convince him to spend a year with me in Toronto, but that's part of him making his own decision as a young man. I would love the opportunity of seeing him every day and having a reason to not sleep in my office.

I'm so proud of who my sons are and know they will grow up to live their own lives and not be like me. As far as preparing them for the negative aspects of life, it's a hard role for a parent to tell a child too much and scare him or her. When I was a kid you didn't have to be worried about guns in schools, AIDS, or violence. I don't know if there are truly more threats now or if we just hear about more events to scare parents. But, I try to give them a taste of what to be careful of, especially when we're traveling. I'm more like the tiger that's been in the jungle – I'm going to see every little thing that moves – they're more like the deer.

My sons are the one thing I can retreat to in my life as a constant feed, and they reenergize me. What gives me great joy is to think that I have a chance to do what I set out to do and simply make life easier for the next generation. The time I spend with them has really helped me how to understand and coach kids like Tracy McGrady. I've learned to let him be a kid when he wants to be a kid, rather than always force him to conform to my attitude or be serious about life.

Tracy can do some things that make me laugh and reminds me of Cris, in that a man can have a lot of fun and still be responsible to his sport. Tracy's so talented he doesn't understand. In a game he'll do something so foolish and walk over to me and

say he knows he did something so wrong but beg to stay in the game. It makes me laugh. Well, sometimes I do take him out of the game, but I understand that this organization needs me to have faith in him growing up.

The beauty of coaching is I feel I can handle all the different personalities, given my experience as the older brother of six and a father of three. My sons help me relate to the guys on the team in a sensitive joyous way, rather than just be a father figure or leader. Still, having children has completed me in a way I never thought possible and I thank them for their special gifts.

"If men do not keep on speaking terms with children,
they cease to be men and merely machines
for eating and for earning money."

JOHN UPDIKE (AUTHOR)

DO YOU HAVE CHILDREN OR WANT CHILDREN IN YOUR LIFE?
IF YOU HAVE CHILDREN, ARE YOU RESPONSIBLE FOR THEM
FINANCIALLY, EMOTIONALLY AND OTHER WAYS?
DO YOU UNDERSTAND YOUR ROLE IN HELPING TO PREPARE
THE NEXT GENERATION?
DO YOU HELP YOUR CHILDREN TO CONTRIBUTE TO
THEIR COMMUNITIES?
WHAT ARE THE VALUES YOU WISH TO PASS ON
TO YOUR CHILDREN?

"Of all team sports, basketball is by far the most schizophrenic, always struggling to decide whether it is ruled by a collection of individuals or a team of them."

FRANK DEFORD (SPORTSCASTER & AUTHOR)

When to be an Individual & When to be a Team Player

The day before I went to training camp in Los Angeles as a rookie, I got a phone call, as did all the free agents and rookies. It was from Earvin (Magic) Johnson's secretary, saying that he was going to pick us up and take us to dinner. I think we all were more than a little surprised.

Magic became an example for me in many ways; his physical commitment, his self-discipline, and certainly that he was a great player. But, here he was responsible enough to make everyone else feel comfortable, even the guys who weren't going to make the team. He took us to dinner and out after for awhile, but left us at about 10 that night. The next morning, there he was, having just won a championship series and Most Valuable Player three months earlier, coming back from a four mile run before we even went to training camp. That was amazing to me and that entire bus ride to training camp, I thought about his magic blend

of being a striking individual as well a team player.

Then, after the first practice at the training camp in Palm Springs, we all had to run a mile, including Magic. It must have been 100 degrees at 1 in the afternoon and I was making a huge effort, as I wanted to make the team. I was running as hard as possible and still couldn't catch Magic. He was a fierce competitor every day – and every day he wanted his team to win. I made the team that year and every evening when dinner was ready, his cook would call me and the other rookie and we'd go over and eat with Magic. He always treated my family and me like his family, and I admire him totally.

He also would never complain about the coaching or the plays or the offense. Magic would never say a word – he'd just run in and execute and for him, it was winning. It didn't make any difference what offense he was running. He could be a strong individual but he also knew when to be a team player.

It's a similar situation now with outstanding players such as Vince Carter. They may think it's unfair, but as I've explained to them, the most talented guys must be the most responsible. That's the way I learned the game. Then I go to the pros and the first day Magic Johnson's there. My whole rookie year I don't play much, but every time he eats, I eat. Magic didn't have to welcome me like that, but he made a point of trying to welcome me to the team. He was and still is, an individual, a team player and a good man.

The young guys who are on our team now are a great group. They have good character, good manners, good attitudes and have been raised by good families. The tough part is their coach doesn't listen to all the hype about them! I've got to get them ready for opponents and encourage them to work as a team. This team focus stems from coaching children. I found those kids who understood the true value of teamwork were less likely to quit when they weren't given certain positions to play or weren't the star.

In Toronto we decided to go after and keep very talented

guys with character who've played for winning teams. That includes veterans. There is often too much implied on the starting position, and people need to realize each play and position has a reason. Players contribute in different ways, much like in the game of life. The solid veteran Kevin Willis may not be starting now, but he doesn't let ego get in the way as he knows he's contributing to the team and keeping us strong. That hard work is a role model in professionalism. An actor may get the public glory, but the scriptwriter, the set designer and sound technicians each play a part in creating a wonderful film.

One of the first things I did at the start of the 99/00 season was meet with the veteran players to clear the air and hear their concerns. I also believe veteran players have much to teach younger players. Whether they like it or not, I think they are role models, much like older to younger siblings. We all need to realize we have common goals of winning a title. When you have a veteran player, he isn't just a veteran who brings experience. He's seen it all, and while we emphasize individual talent and competence, we also need to focus on our unique individual roles to get us all where we want to be – and that's the playoffs. We achieved this in the 99/00 season, the first in the Toronto Raptors history. To achieve that, we have to be cohesive and direct our energy to the team goals.

However, there are players in the league who don't care about reaching the playoffs. They know they're getting a guaranteed salary and like the idea of being off every April. There's nothing significant about the amount of money you're going to earn in the playoffs. It's not worth the two extra months from a financial standpoint. There are guys who just want to play their allotted games, go out every night, and want to get a big new contract. Then there are the other guys, who all they've ever known is to be playing at the end of the year all the way up the ladder. That dedication requires a greater commitment of being a great team player and of being a great individual.

The day they wake up and say they'll take the responsibility

of being the first guy out on the floor and being the first in all the drills, is the day that Toronto will have a great team. Because, that's the day we've got a group of individuals who can act like leaders when they understand they can lead in different ways.

I never forgot how hard you have to work if you want to get ahead and this work ethic was instilled early in me and reiterated by guys like Magic. What he did for me as an individual and as a team player, when he didn't even know me, was memorable. I absolutely wish he didn't have HIV so he could do all the things he wants and see his kids grow up and I love him even more for being up front about it. In professional sports, you stay away from judging morality and I believe that if you love someone, if you're going to care about someone doing well, you're there for him or her all the time, no matter what. If there's anything I can ever do for him or his kids, it's done. I'm trying to return the respect to my players that I hadn't even earned from Magic that rookie year.

I know the focus the past couple of decades has been on being an individual and individual rights, but I think people need to understand the significance of how hard work does pay off individually, yet also contributes to the whole objective of any defined group or relationship.

"Try not to be a man of success, but a man of value."

ALBERT EINSTEIN (SCIENTIST)

HOW DO YOU EXPRESS YOUR INDIVIDUAL TALENTS?
WHAT ARE THE WAYS YOU CONTRIBUTE TO A GROUP QUEST, FOR EXAMPLE; IN A WORK GROUP, SCHOOL PROJECT OR SPORTS TEAM?
DO YOU KNOW WHEN TO BE AN INDIVIDUAL AND WHEN TO BE A TEAM PLAYER?
ARE YOU WORRIED YOU'LL GIVE UP YOUR INDIVIDUALISM IF YOU FOCUS ON TEAM GOALS?

"If you don't have confidence, you'll always find a way not to win."

CARL LEWIS (ATHLETE)

Winning & Losing

Everyone's heard that old platitude that it doesn't matter if you win or lose, it's how you play the game. Well, in professional sports, that's not quite true. The whole point is to win, just as in the business world. If you're a salesperson and don't win the big deals very often over your company's competitor, you don't last long. If you're on a debate team at school and don't win, you may still get the practice and experience, but you don't win the competition. The concept of enjoyment of the game and sportsmanship is important to impart especially for children, but our society's reward system is based on winning the game. That's not just a 20th century development; winning has always been critical, whether war, conflict or professional awards.

There are calls I've disputed and there are days I've said I've had enough. And there is certainly a pressure to win – just watch for a slump of three losing games and people are predicting a huge slide. But competition does encourage children to learn skills from

their peers, to stretch their talents and to take pride in their achievements. But I do think while the rewards are obvious, sport still tries to promote a fair game, especially to young people. You can see this in the Olympic games where it's customary for teams to line up at the end of the game and shake hands.

Of course we all want to win – it gives us motivation, pumps everyone up and besides monetary rewards, there is the thrill of knowing all the elements of hard work have paid off. People share in victory, but often disappear in defeat. There's no feeling like it when you're on a winning streak – except to realize it's a fleeting feeling. And it's dreadful to look up in the stands and see fans fleeing the game near the end. Although we don't win every night, we notice and appreciate those faithful fans who stick it out to the end.

Winning on the court is one thing, but I also want to win with our fans and connect the players more with the fan base, especially with kids and blue collar workers in all parts of Canada and our fans in the United States. I want us to play a tough brand of basketball that will turn the east side of the country on, will excite the west and all the small towns and big cities in between. Although we can't play in all those towns, with an improved television broadcast we feel we appeal to a unique fan base with great sensibilities and support. With basketball now having a home base in the country, we feel proud to be promoting a new game to Canada on a home soil.

When I was given the job in Toronto, it was really in the gutter of teams. I needed a group of young guys with the energy to match the energy I had so we could climb the mountain together. Although I was an assistant coach in the NBA, I was used to coaching high school basketball and feeding off the excitement of the players. So, I looked at this new team and the players compared to that. The team being at the bottom of the basement made it a perfect job as it allowed me to work.

I wrote to thank the owners for giving me the job, saying that they would not regret their faith in me. I think that they've stuck

their heads out and I appreciate it. They purchased an asset as an investment, that was new to supporters in Toronto, but now I think they get a lot of compliments on what has developed with their team. And, the important thing is, although we accomplished a lot in wins, we have also helped our players and the city understand that we are here to stay as part of this city and country. We're a young team and it will take a few years to mature this foundation.

It's not going to be easy and we're going to get bruised along the way, but the performance these guys put in the 98/99 season showed we're serious players – missing the playoffs by one game was a pretty good showing. From that, we understood there was a lot of work to do in the off-season in the summer, so we evaluated, watched tapes, compiled player reports and worked on strengthening skills.

For the 99/00 season we decided to be strictly business. I expected to deal with the players in a professional business-like manner and I wanted them to be aggressive and go after chances – they have so much talent it was my chance to help make the talent better; that helps them grow and come back stronger every year. The raw and developed talent that is out there these days is staggering.

I think the new marketing idea is to win. I don't mean that facetiously, just that we had a groundbreaking season in 98/99 and became recognized within Toronto and in the NBA as a team in contention. We came into the 99/00 as the team to watch and we did our homework to ensure we had a good year and went to the playoffs. As head coach I have a wonderful opportunity to support and guide the players to produce a consistent winning team. And if I don't have any faith in them, just how are they going to have faith in themselves?

I'm trying for the fans, the assistant coaches, the marketing and sales staff, our management – I'm trying to make their job easier. I'm trying to create winners for everyone who's dependent

on me, excite our fans and create champions. So while it is important how you play the game, winning is a whole lot better than losing.

"One of the problems I have witnessed with bad sportsmanship is definitely the parents as spectators. I have seen many parents argue and even badmouth the coaches because their son or daughter didn't have enough playing time or dislike the way the coach teaches."

KELLY RICE (8TH GRADE STUDENT, NEW JERSEY, USA)

WHAT DOES IT TAKE TO WIN?
ARE YOU GRACIOUS WHEN YOU LOSE?
WHEN OTHERS WIN, DO YOU CONGRATULATE THEM?
WHAT DO YOU LEARN FROM LOSING?

Books I Recommend:

THE REST OF US
BY STEPHEN BIRMINGHAM
An inspiring account of history and the integration of Eastern European Jews in America. This book made me understand the sacrifices one generation must make for the following generation.

MAN'S SEARCH FOR MEANING
BY VIKTOR FRANKEL
How inner purpose drives individuals faced with even the most difficult of conflict and circumstances.

THE COLLECTED POEMS OF
LANGSTON HUGHES
ARNOLD RAMPERSAD (ED.)
A fine collection of the celebrated Black American literary master, including I, Too, Sing America.

THE SACKETT SERIES
BY LOUIS L'AMOUR
The stories of the Sackett family, as they see opportunity in leaving their country to create a new home.

THE GIVER
BY LOIS LOWRY
A coming of age story where a boy discovers the disturbing truth about his new utopian world and struggles against its hypocrisy.

THE ART OF WAR
SUN TZU: TRANSLATED BY
SAMUEL B. GRIFFITH
Based on 2,000 year old writings on military strategy, this book is now a business classic.

MANDELA: AN ILLUSTRATED
AUTOBIOGRAPHY
BY NELSON MANDELA
A poignant account of Nelson Mandela's struggle to end apartheid and become an inspirational political and world leader.

THEIR EYES WERE
WATCHING GOD
BY ZORA NEALE HURSTON
An American classic of the remarkable emotion-filled life of a woman and the journey of her spirit as she finds her voice.

Notes